Tax Guide 301

DECISIONS WHEN RETIRING

by

Holmes F. Crouch
Tax Specialist

Published by

Allyear Tax Guides

20484 Glen Brae Drive
Saratoga, CA 95070

ISBN 0-944817-37-8

LCCN 97-73075

Printed in U.S.A.

Series 300

Retirees and Estates

Tax Guide 301

DECISIONS WHEN RETIRING

For other titles in print, see page 224.

The author: **Holmes F. Crouch**
For more about the author, see page 221.

PREFACE

If you are a knowledge-seeking **taxpayer** looking for information, this book can be helpful to you. It is designed to be read — from cover to cover — in less than eight hours. Or, it can be "skim-read" in about 30 minutes.

Either way, you are treated to **tax knowledge** . . . *beyond the ordinary*. The "beyond" is that which cannot be found in IRS publications, FedWorld on-line services, tax software programs, or on CD-ROMs.

Taxpayers have different levels of interest in a selected subject. For this reason, this book starts with introductory fundamentals and progresses onward. You can verify the progression by chapter and section in the table of contents. In the text, "applicable law" is quoted in pertinent part. Key phrases and key tax forms are emphasized. Real-life examples are given . . . in down-to-earth style.

This book has 12 chapters. This number provides depth without cross-subject rambling. Each chapter starts with a head summary of meaningful information.

To aid in your skim-reading, informative diagrams and tables are placed strategically throughout the text. By leafing through page by page, reading the summaries and section headings, and glancing at the diagrams and tables, you can get a good handle on the matters covered.

Effort has been made to update and incorporate all of the latest tax law changes that are *significant* to the title subject. However, "beyond the ordinary" does not encompass every conceivable variant of fact and law that might give rise to protracted dispute and litigation. Consequently, if a particular statement or paragraph is crucial to your own specific case, you are urged to seek professional counseling. Otherwise, the information presented is general and is designed for a broad range of reader interests.

The Author

INTRODUCTION

As an occupationally active person, sooner or later you will retire. You may retire early (in your 50s), normally (in your 60s), or late (in your 70s). At whatever age you do so, there are many decisions to make. Some will be major (like selling your home and moving out of state); some will be irreversible (such as choosing among your retirement plan options); but most will require a "shift in thinking" from one lifestyle to another.

Unlike the recent past, people are living longer in retirement these days. When the Social Security System was instituted in the mid-1930s, life expectancy averaged between 62 and 67 years. Today, the range is 75 to 78 years . . . with 85 being the most practical assumption for full retirement planning.

Aside from living longer, the lifestyle change in retirement stems from **three given facts**, namely: (1) less income, (2) inflation, and (3) taxes. All three impact on the decisions that you have to make.

Living on less income means that you have to adjust downward anywhere from 20% to 40% of your pre-retirement income. Can you do this? If not, we have some suggestions how you can, depending on whether you are employed, unemployed, or self-employed at the time.

While actively working, adjustments for inflation are (more or less) automatic. Not so in retirement. Most pension, annuity, and IRA plans disregard inflation altogether. Even social security is "subindexed" relative to the real rate of inflation. This means that you have to pay closer attention to your discretionary nest egg. We offer some suggestions in this regard through low-cost mutual funds, working part-time, deferring IRA withdrawals (until after 70$1/2$), and not too hastily selling your home.

Perhaps the most overriding factor that you will face in retirement is: **Incessant taxes.** As recently as prior to 1980, retirees could look forward to paying considerably less taxes than during their working years. No more! Big Government and the IRS (another government) have their revenue guns focused as severely on retirees as on nonretirees. Social security benefits, once sacrosanct, are now taxed. Private activity municipal bonds, once tax free, are now taxed. Unemployment compensation, once tax exempt, is now taxed. Capital gains are now complicated with new rules on stocks, bonds, mutual fund shares, collectibles, and real estate held for investment. The qualifying threshold for medical expense deductions has been raised. All of these adjustments automatically "bump up" the tax rates on other retirement, investment, and part-time income. Because of this, there are "estimated" taxes to prepay. In addition, there is *double taxation* on "nonresident state" income for those retirees living in a state other than that in which they have real or tangible property. The overall reality is: ***Retirement is no longer a safe haven from taxation***. We address this subject quite thoroughly in this book.

We devote an entire chapter to the options you have between ages 62 and 70 when applying for social security benefits . . . and continuing to work part-time thereafter. If you are a "wealthy retiree" [Tier 1 = $25,000/$32,000; Tier 2 = $34,000/$44,000], you may be better off postponing application until age 70.

Major changes in national policy towards retirement will occur after year 2000. For starters, eligibility for social security will "shift forward" by two years. Additionally, Congress is expecting that more workers will participate in self-directed and employer-sponsored private plans to reduce the strains on social security and medicare. Are you — and your spouse — prepared to bear some of this burden on your own?

We offer thoughts on ways to convert (and consume) any substantial equity that you have built up in your home over your 30 to 50 years of ownership working life. In the process, we touch on the "old" $125,000 exclusion-of-gain rule which you probably know about (and may even have already used). We'll also introduce to you the "new" (post-August 5, 1997) $500,000 exclusion-of-gain rule when selling your final residence. Do you know about reverse mortgages, life estates, and "twilight exchanges"?

So, when you attend those pre-retirement, post-retirement, and wealth preservation seminars that you are invited to, we urge that you take along a copy of this book. It will serve as a useful source from which you can think of questions to ask, to further enhance your retirement decision-making.

CONTENTS

vii

1

PRE-RETIREMENT PREPARATION

Most Reasonably Healthy Persons Can Expect To Live 15 To 25 Years In Retirement (Depending, Of Course, On Age When Retiring). Because Of This "Living Longer" Timespan On Reduced Income (About 30% Less), Adequate Forethought And Preparation Are Required. Your First Decision Is To "Start Thinking" About Retirement Matters 3 To 5 Years In Advance. Select A Target Age Or Year, And Allow At Least Two Years For RETIREMENT ACCLIMATION Before Selling Your Last Employment Home. Get Out Of Debt And Prepare For Inflation Erosion Of Your Nest Egg To About 50% Of Its Initial Value.

Retiring is a major phase change in life that requires good preparation and forethought. It is analogous to that of a graduate from an educational institution being launched into the national workforce. Instead, of course, you are being "delaunched" from the workforce. Just as one prepares for his occupation of choice, so must he prepare for his retirement of choice.

For analogous thinking purposes, use age 85 as an actuarial reference. You, yourself, may not live this long or you may live longer. Whether you do or not is not the point. It is a demographic fact that people are living longer these days. This is particularly true for those who are in average good health for their age (no major sickness, illness, or disability). Consequently, some actuarial reference is needed so that you can gauge on your own the number of years you'll be in retirement.

Using age 85 as an actuarial reference (we'll present actuarial figures later), suppose you decided to retire at age 60. This means that your retirement lifespan would approximate 25 years. If you retired at 65, you'd have approximately 20 years of retirement life. If you retired at age 70, there would be 15 years left. In other words, you should count on somewhere between 15 and 25 years of probable retirement life . . . say, 20 years on average.

It is because of this number of years in retirement that you should start thinking about the phase change before you. Note that we are urging that you simply "start thinking" about retirement matters. This alone is a decision. The decision is not to make any final decision; the decision is to start thinking about what you'll have to decide on later.

Start Talking to Retirees

A good way to get "start thinking" information on retirement matters is to search out and talk to persons who have already retired. These are those who have stepped beyond that phase-change threshold and cannot go back. Their own personal experiences become a delightful source of valuable information that you will not find elsewhere.

Talk to early retirees (those retiring in their 50s), normal retirees (those retiring in their 60s), and late retirees (those retiring in their 70s). You want to talk to different retiree age groups, economic groups, activity groups, and health groups. For us, a "retiree" is a person who has no full-time occupation for livelihood purposes. He/she may be a volunteer worker, or a part-time worker, or an occasional consultant. But none of this is for basic livelihood purposes. The basic livelihood of a retiree comes from pension plans, social security, and personal savings.

As you (and your spouse) talk to these retirees (and their spouses), show a genuine interest in their retirement affairs. Tell them that you are starting to think about the day when you will retire. You want to get some ideas and recommendations from them. Ask questions in the most general of terms. For example, you might ask: "How do you like retirement?" "What are the three most difficult decisions you had to make?" "What do you do with all of your leisure time?" "If you could go back and cross the threshold again, what would you do differently?" Try to focus your questions on matters such as living standards, personal finances, health insurance, travel plans, hobby interests, part-time work, home sales, and so on.

Your objective is not to probe too deeply into their personal affairs and finances. All you want to know is what general retirement decisions were of most concern to them. You want to get a feel for what they had to go through to make their final (or semi-final) decisions. Did they pull up stakes and move to an entirely new community? Or, did they stay put and develop new interests for their retirement years?

Surely, among your circle of family, friends, neighbors, business associates, church members, club groups, and other organizations, you can find an ample supply of eager and perhaps not-so-eager retirees to talk to. Our recommendation is, at the minimum, to talk openly and frankly to between 5 and 10 retirees. You want to gain as broad a perspective as possible on the diversity of options you can expect to encounter. Preferably, seek out those who have retired within the past five years. After five years or so of retirement, medical problems and grandchildren tend to dominate conversation; the practicalities of decision making fade from concern.

Set a Target Age

After talking to a fair number of retirees, you will be developing a consensus of your own as to what is a good age to retire. A "target age" is a tentative selection only. It may change based on the insistence of your employer, the economy, or nature (as brought on by illness or disability). Nevertheless, you need to set for yourself a specific target age with reference to which you make certain retirement and post-retirement decisions.

For initial reference purposes, age 62 is often used as the consensus age for retirement. Why this particular age? Answer: Because of our social security system.

All workers who are "fully insured" under the Social Security Act can apply for and commence collecting social security benefits at age 62. Not that they necessarily want to, or need to, or must. But it is an age that, if you were planning on social security for supplementing your other retirement income sources, you need to work towards for planning your goals and achievements.

Under present law (which changes at the year 2000), one cannot receive *full benefits* from social security until he/she attains age 65. So, if you target age 62 for retirement, the benefits that you would receive would be 80% of those that you would receive at age 65. Persons who delay retirement until age 70 would receive approximately 120% of the benefits they would receive at 65.

For persons attaining age 62 in the year 2000 and thereafter, the full benefits age shifts forward from 65 to 67 by year 2022. We suspect that before then the delayed benefits will also shift forward from 70 to 72. All of this "shifting forward" business is political recognition of the fact that people are living (and working) longer these days, and that the social security system is coming under greater and greater financial pressure.

Most persons retire voluntarily between the ages of 55 and 75. Thus, if you have no set age in mind at this point in time, assume age 65 with the expectation of shifting it forward. By shifting your target age slightly, it allows more time to live more comfortably in your pre-retirement years. It also gives you a little more time to pre-test the marketability of your occupational expertise, should you desire to work part-time in your retirement years.

Prepare for Lower Income

There is one universal reality of retirement that you must face up front. You'll have to learn to live on less income. Typically, one's retirement income is 60% to 80% of his pre-retirement sources. No retirement plan, be it employer sponsored, government sponsored, or self sponsored, or any combination thereof, provides for 100% of your pre-retirement income. This is a given. Consequently, you have to prepare to live on less income.

It is true that in retirement certain expenses will be less. This is particularly true of mortgage payments, car payments, working expenses, credit card items, children's education, etc. But it is also true that certain expenses will increase. These include such items as health insurance, medical costs, travel, and other leisure-necessitated expenditures. These increases will further increase simply because of inflationary effects. During your active occupational years, your personal compensation was more or less automatically adjusted for inflation. Except for social security, there is no automatic adjustment for inflation in your retirement years. Because government statistics on inflation rates are not always reliable, you should plan on an average real rate of inflation of about 5% per year.

The overall effect is that, in retirement, there **will** be less income for you to live on. For target thinking and preparation purposes, consider that your retirement income (from all sources) will be 70% of your pre-retirement income. Can you live on 30% less income than you are currently receiving? If you can't now, you'll have no choice after retirement. This may well become the most difficult post-retirement adjustment you will have to make. Better prepare for it before tomorrow comes.

Having to live on lower income is a fact of retirement life. This fact is the very reason why we suggested earlier that you start thinking — we mean, **really** start thinking — about retirement some three to five years before your targeted age. More than just thinking, you have to start doing something. That "something" is: Start living on lower income *before* your retirement. Are you up to this?

Our recommendation is that you incrementally **reduce** your spending habits each year, as you get closer and closer to retirement. For example, suppose you decide to start adjusting to lower living standards five years before retirement. In each of those five years, you would reduce your spending habits by the following percentages:

1st year	10%)	
2nd year	20%)	
3rd year	30%)	Average reduction is 30% per year
4th year	40%)	
5th year	50%)	

If five years is too long a "torture time," use three years for your spending reduction adjustments. Make the adjustments each year as follows:

1st year	20%)	
2nd year	30%)	Average reduction is 30% per year
3rd year	40%)	

Our observation has been that it is amazing how much you can save in three to five years pre-retirement time, if you put your heart and soul into it. You will not have sacrificed in vain. You add those savings to your retirement nest egg . . . to be spent later. This is what we call pre-retirement *spend down* for post-retirement *spend more*. We try to illustrate this concept for you in Figure 1.1. The achievement in Figure 1.1 is not automatic; it is something you have to decide to do on your own.

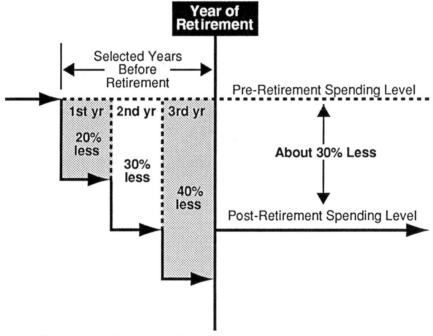

Fig. 1.1 - Pre-Retirement "Adjustment Steps" for Spending Less

Max Out Employer Plans

If voluntary spend-down efforts are too much for you, there is another less painful way to accomplish nearly the same end. That is, you "max out" all of your *elective contributions* to your employer retirement plans. These plans vary in form and eligibility requirements. They are variously called pension plans, profit-sharing plans, stock bonus plans, annuity plans, savings plans, or deferred compensation plans. Most of these plans provide for some amount of voluntary contributions at the election of each employee.

In general, your voluntary contributions are limited to the *lower of* a fixed percentage of your compensation (5% to 10% or less) or a fixed amount ($8,000 to $10,000 or less). These elective amounts vary from plan to plan, and from employer to employer. These variations are not due to the whims of employers but to the barrage of tax law changes and regulations added subsequent to the Employee Retirement Income Security Act (ERISA) in 1974. As a result, today fewer and fewer companies are offering traditional-type pension plans and are opting instead for deferred compensation plans. All of such plans have statutory limits for "maxing out."

Our recommendation is that you contact the administrator of each plan in which you are a participant, and find out exactly how much more you can contribute. Then force yourself to contribute up to the maximum that your deferred compensation arrangement allows. By doing so, you get a two-fold advantage. One: You get an off-the-top income tax deduction for your elective contributions. Two: You are building up retirement savings which are tax deferred.

Consolidate Your IRAs

As you probably already know, the acronym IRA stands for Individual Retirement Account. It was enacted in 1974 and became effective as IRC Section 408 commencing in 1975. The idea was to encourage individual taxpayers to commence a long-term savings program for their own retirement. It was a form of national recognition that the social security system alone would not be sufficient to support workers in their retirement years. Initially, elective contributions to IRA accounts were limited to $1,500 per year, and were deductible against one's total income. In 1982, the amount was increased to $2,000 but many new restrictions were imposed.

The IRA savings concept as an elective supplement to social security is truly a good idea. But Congress, the IRS, and financial institutions have botched things up terribly. It is now a complicated and confusing mess of contributory IRAs, spousal IRAs, partial IRAs, nondeductible IRAs, SEP IRAs, and rollover IRAs. There are restrictions and limitations depending on a contributor's total income and on whether or not he (or his spouse) is a participant in an employer-sponsored or other elective-deferral plan. Most of the confusion arises over computing the amount of partial IRAs allowed, reporting one's after-tax basis in nondeductible IRAs, and the disharmonies of computer matching that arise when "rolling over" into and out of various IRA and pension accounts.

Meanwhile, as part of your pre-retirement preparation effort, you should consolidate all of your various IRA and pension-type accounts into one single IRA **rollover account**.

The concept we have in mind is depicted in Figure 1.2. Note that each rollover is initiated by an IRA "Transfer Authorization" form by each financial institution involved.

IRA "rollovers," if properly handled, are treated as tax-free exchanges under the provisions of Section 408(d)(3) of the Internal Revenue Code. The following types of rollovers are recognized by this section, namely:

(1) The transfer of assets from one IRA to another IRA.
(2) The transfer of assets from a qualified pension, profit-sharing, stock bonus, or annuity to an IRA.
(3) The transfer of assets from a tax-sheltered annuity plan (403(b)) to an IRA.
(4) The transfer of assets from a termination trust to an IRA.
(5) The transfer of assets from a qualified deferred compensation plan (such as 401(k), SEP) to an IRA.

When making a consolidation-type rollover, you should be aware of the following rules:

1. Roll over only the "before tax" portions of your account. If, mistakenly, you roll over your after-tax contributions, you

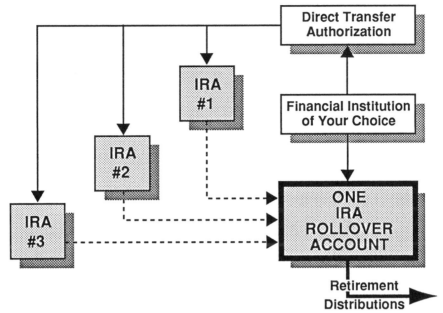

Fig. 1.2 - Concept of Consolidating your IRAs Before Retirement

are subject to excess contribution and premature withdrawal penalties.

2. If you make an "indirect" rollover (where the before-tax money passes through your hands), you must complete the transaction within 60 days. You are limited to one such rollover per year, and are subject to rollover "backup withholding" (up to 30%).

3. If you make a "direct" rollover, called a trustee-to-trustee transfer, you can make any number of rollovers in a given year, and you are not subject to backup withholdings.

Prepare for Higher Taxes

Many about-to-be retirees delude themselves into thinking that, because their total income will be lower, their Form 1040 taxes also will be lower. Some even think that they can discontinue filing tax returns altogether. This is a great misconception. In our cradle-to-grave tax information and surveillance society, not only are you likely to pay higher taxes in retirement, but the process will be more frustrating, too. Particularly when you start converting some of your nest-egg assets into cash for consumption and enjoyment.

We'll tell you right now that your year of retirement will probably be your most complicated retirement tax return year. If you are employed at the time, you'll be presented with a number of retirement plan options to consider. All come with tax consequences to one degree or another. In addition, your reportable income will include accumulated vacation time, incentive awards, interests in savings and stock plans, and other forms of retirement benefits. When employees retire, every employer wants to "clean up his books" (so to speak) with respect to each retiree. Usually, you are given a deadline that coincides with the employer's — or the plan administrator's — tax return filings . . . on a fiscal year basis. Rarely does this deadline coincide with your own calendar year for income tax filings.

If your expected retirement income from all sources exceeds $40,000, you enter a new tax world where you are classed as a "wealthy retiree." This means that up to 85% of your social security benefits may be taxed. In 1984, Congress "saved" the social security system by taxing up to 50% of a retiree's benefits. (Prior to 1984, social security benefits were never taxed.) In 1994, Congress again "saved" the system by increasing the taxable portion to 85%. This one fact alone will increase your after-retirement taxes.

Clear Up Unresolved Matters

Many about-to-be retirees slip into retirement without aggressively clearing up unresolved matters accumulated during employment. Such matters may include unpaid back taxes and unfiled tax returns. You should have your tax records organized and completed for at least five years immediately preceding your retirement year. If you don't have these records, you must do your very best to reconstruct them. You simply do not want to face retirement with any tax matters hanging over your head. Emotionally — and financially, too — these matters can drain you when you are most vulnerable. Taxes are forever: retirement notwithstanding.

The same is true if you're involved in litigation of any form. If you have "tail ends" of disputive issues such as divorce, civil lawsuits, insurance claims, consumer complaints, traffic tickets, etc., try to compromise and settle each issue . . . somehow. Attorneys and judges are like tax collectors. They have no compassion for retirees. They offer no discounts or leniency, even though they themselves may be of retirement age.

Try also to settle up your credit cards and other outstanding bills. Cut back on your expenditures so that you can adapt to a "prompt payment" policy once you have retired. As a retiree, you want to be in a position to pay cash (within 30 days) for all purchases that you make. Once in voluntary retirement, your goal is to be debt free.

One of your major pre-retirement goals, if you own a home, is to get your mortgage paid off. If necessary — and it probably will be — dip into your retirement savings to do so. Check with your mortgage company on this. Request a statement of the exact payoff amount and the effective date thereof. Pay it off and request prompt delivery of the **Deed of Reconveyance.** The term "prompt delivery" probably means six months or so. You want the reconveyance deed properly recorded in public records where your property is located. While this recording is in process, check to see if there are any liens or other legal attachments to your home which you may not know about. Visit a local title company in your area, cite your APN (Assessor's Parcel Number), and request that your APN be pulled up on its title-search computer screen. If a fee is involved, pay it. If you are really preparing to retire, you want your home totally free and clear.

"Stay Put" for Two Years

Many about-to-be retirees think that one of the first things they have to do upon retirement is to sell their home and move on. Our advice, based on many observations of others, is: DO NOT SELL your home immediately upon retirement. Selling immediately can be a big mistake financially and emotionally. There will be enough turmoil in your life when you change from employment to retirement. Do not add to this turmoil by selling, moving, storing, and getting rid of some of your lifelong possessions.

We recommend strongly that you "stay put" — stay the course — in your present home for at least two years after you have retired. In terms of your remaining actuarial life expectancy, two years is a short time. Besides you probably have a number of unfinished projects and improvements around the house that you want to do. You may also want to visit your children, grandchildren, relatives, and friends who live some distance from you. We depict this important waiting period concept in Figure 1.3.

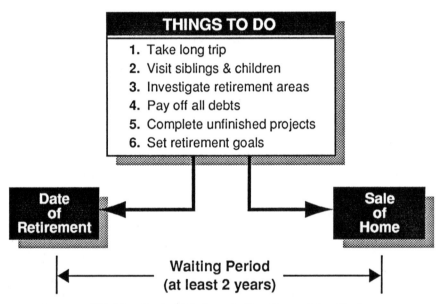

Fig. 1.3 - "Waiting Period" Before Selling Home After Retirement

The tax rules on selling your home (after age 55) allow up to two full years of absence, while still retaining its tax character as your personal residence. During this time you can vacate your home entirely, let friends and relatives house-sit it, or rent it to others. You can do this for two years while traveling around the country, or the world, visiting all the popular retirement communities.

If, ultimately, you do plan to sell your home and move to a retirement community, why not try renting there first? Too many just-retireds move too fast to one retirement community, only to find out that they do not like the place. For some reason they don't "fit in." It is better to rent at or near one, two, or three such communities before you really settle down at a selected one for good. Actually, less than one in five retirees moves to a permanent retirement community. Most either stay in their last employment home or sell and buy a smaller home (condo, apartment, town house, mobile home) in the area with which they are familiar, and where their family and friends reside.

Study Your Actuarial Odds

Going into retirement is not the end of the road. There's a new road of 15 to 20 years before you. How far you go down this new road depends on your state of health and state of mind at the time of your retirement. You want to assess both in your last pre-retirement (employment) year. Each becomes a reference marker for your pathway ahead.

In your last year of employment, you want to arrange for a complete physical examination. You want to know the state of your health from head to toe. You want documentation of your "vital signs" (heart, blood, lungs, eyes, teeth, bones, internals, etc.) and all the ailments you may have. Ideally you would like a medical prognosis of what your health future holds. Very few medical practitioners will make any forecasts for you. Usually, they will tell you that in due time "nature's signals" will come forth. This means that you will have to study your own actuarial odds.

Barring any serious disability or life-threatening illness, you can study actuarial tables of your life expectancy and plan on living to that age. You realize, of course, that actuarial tables are simply statistical averages of people deaths. The averages developed are based on deaths from natural causes: not on accidents, or murders. Said tables can provide a reasonable prognosis of about when you can expect to die.

The IRS has prepared single-life actuarial tables for taxing annuity contracts. We present this IRS data in rearranged form in

Figure 1.4. The "rearrangement" is that we added to your age at retirement the IRS's actuarial factor to come up with your age at death. Note that the life expectancy of females is, on average, two or three years more than that of men. Over 80% of all centenarians (persons of age 100 or more) are women.

AGE AT RETIREMENT	LIFE EXPECTANCY			
	MALE		FEMALE	
	Actuarial Factor	Age at Death	Actuarial Factor	Age at Death
50	25.5	75.5	29.6	79.6
55	21.7	76.7	25.5	80.5
60	18.2	78.2	21.7	81.7
65	15.0	80.0	18.2	83.2
70	12.1	82.1	15.0	85.0
75	9.6	84.6	12.1	87.1
80	7.5	87.5	9.6	89.6
85	5.7	90.7	7.5	92.5
90	4.2	94.2	5.7	95.7
95	3.1	98.1	4.2	99.2
///////	IRS Reg. 1.72-9 : Annuity Tables			///////

Fig. 1.4 - Life Expectancy From IRS's Actuarial Tables

There is a paradoxical message in Figure 1.4. It is: The later you retire, the longer you live! Sounds odd, doesn't it? For example, if you retire at 60 as a male, you can expect to live to age 78. If you retire at 70, you should live to age 82. If you retire at 80, you should live to age 87 — almost 10 years longer than if you retire at 60.

What is the reason for living longer as you get older? There are two theories: heredity and mental activity.

Heredity and ancestral longevity are good indicators of your life expectancy. Longevity is definitely related to genealogical genes handed down from generation to generation. You may want to make inquiry into your own family history on this.

The other longevity theory has to do with one's mental state of purpose. There is a lot of leisure time in retirement. It mounts and mounts after several years in the retirement mode. How do you use your leisure time? Do you use it strictly for leisure, or do you intersperse it with a constructive agenda of something you want to accomplish before passing on? Most people who are in their 80s and beyond, who are vigorous and healthy, have some "active agenda" which seems to drive them on. In your pre-retirement preparatory thoughts, you ought to think a little about what your active agenda might be.

Inflation Reality

We all know that monetary inflation is a fact of life. One dollar today is not going to be worth one dollar 5, 10, or 15 years from now. It will be less, depending on the average rate of inflation over the course of your retirement years. How much less? That all depends. So, let's make some illustrative assumptions.

Suppose you retire at age 65. If you do so, it is a reasonable assumption that you can expect to live to about age 80 (see Figure 1.4). That's 15 years of retirement consumption of money. Let's assume that the average rates of inflation over these 15 years are 3%, 5%, and 7%. On these assumptions, one dollar 15 years from now would be worth—

64 cents @ 3% average inflation
48 cents @ 5%   "   "
36 cents @ 7%   "   "

So, figure roughly that your nest-egg savings will buy only about 50% of what they would have bought when you first retired.

And the irony is that, while inflation is eating away at your nest egg, your expenditure needs for medical and hospice-type care will increase as you advance further into retirement. There is a way (at least partially) to compensate for this divergence in income needs (they go up) and the value of money (it goes down). This is to commit to a long-term growth-type investment program shortly after you retire. By "long term" we mean five years or longer.

Low-Cost Mutual Funds

While one is actively employed, the "in thing" often is to have a financial counselor help supervise your retirement nest egg. The presumption is that, while employed, you are too busy to devote much of your own time to investment matters. In contrast, in retirement you'll have ample time to do much of the supervision on your own. There's a ton of self-help computer software programs, investor advisory newsletters, and retirement planner handbooks on the market to educate you.

If you are inclined to want to make investment decisions on your own, there is one guidebook source that we recommend very highly. It's a good, comprehensive beginners-type manual titled: *Investor's Guide to Low-Cost Mutual Funds*. It is published and distributed by the—

Mutual Fund Education Alliance
The Association of No-Load Funds
Department 0148
P.O. Box 419263
Kansas City, MO 64193-0148
Phone: (816) 454-9422

For the grand sum of about $15 per copy, this guidebook is the best investment you could ever make. It is updated annually in April and lists more than 1,000 different investments available from the leading mutual fund management companies. It is intended for those who want to make their own investment decisions by purchasing mutual funds directly without a broker. It profiles the major no-load mutual funds, discusses the various fund types, tells you how to control your assets, reviews mutual fund regulations, and gives pointers on making the right investment choices.

As our final message in this chapter, you owe it to yourself to become familiar with low-cost mutual funds. You need to do this as a way to enhance your retirement nest egg without its being imprudently depleted by unnecessary fees, commissions, and handling charges. Whether you do so or not is your decision.

2

PREMATURE RETIREMENT WOES

If You Are Severed From Employment In Your Early 50s, You Become A "Premature Retiree." You Face A Crisis In Re-Employment Efforts To Make Up For Lost Savings Towards Normal Retirement. Immediately Commence A 3-IRA Plan, Register With Your State Unemployment Office, Update Your Resumé, And Pursue Temporary Employments Which Offer 401(k) and 408(k) Plans. Try Employment Overseas (Where A $70,000 Earned Income Exclusion Applies), Self-Employment (for 401(c) Plans), And Government Employment (For Its Security Plans). Before Trying To Survive On The Equity In Your Residence, TAP INTO Your Inheritance . . . Delicately.

In Chapter 1, we previewed those preparatory matters associated with normal retirement. By "normal retirement," we mean a person who retires in his mid-60s (62 to 67, say) and who does so voluntarily. He is fully employed or nearly fully employed up until the target age or year that he (more or less) selected for retirement. Although he may have been prodded into retiring at a specific age due to company policy, he is still allowed some flexibility and voluntarism.

By "premature retirement," we mean those persons who are forced to retire from their livelihood employment while still in their 50s. The polite characterization of this situation is called: *early retirement.* A few sweeteners are added to the employer's reduced — much reduced — pension/annuity benefits to make the pushout more palatable. But the bottom line is that one is forced into retirement whether he wants to be retired or not. It is a crisis form of unemployment after working for a company 15, 20, or 25 years.

In the orgy of downsizings sweeping corporate America, there are many premature retirees these days. Said persons are healthy and vigorous; they (usually) are at the peak of their skills and expertise in their chosen employment field. When forced into retirement prematurely, their self-esteem is shattered. They go into a state of shock and depression. They are too young to retire, and too old to be hired readily in the national workforce. They are in a precarious stage where special decisions and strategies are required.

In this chapter, therefore, we want to focus on the special problems and woes of those who have been forced into unemployment in their 50s. Much reorientation of one's talents and resources are required, in order to go forward intelligently . . . and with purpose. That purpose, of course, is the pursuit of all opportunities to maximize one's retirement nest egg before it is financially too late.

"Premature" is under 59$^{1/2}$

Many employers classify early retirees as those of age between 55 and 62. This is the age range where retirement sweeteners sometimes are offered. Rarely are sweeteners offered to employees under 55. Said persons are simply let go and laid off. They are "terminated." When terminated, employers are required to turn over to the affected persons all of their accumulated rights to any pension plan benefits.

Age 55 is used because **some** qualified employee retirement plans permit penalty-free (that is, tax penalty free) distributions when separated from service after attaining age 55. Otherwise, a 10% federal tax penalty applies to distributions from any retirement plan where the recipient is under age 59$^{1/2}$.

Age 62 is used by employers as the upper end of early retirement because social security "kicks in" at that age. That is, it kicks in if the early retiree applies for his social security benefits at that age. Many employer plans are *integrated* with the social security system to give an enhanced figure of what one's retirement benefits would be. What is omitted from these plans is the fact that social security is based on a reduced benefits schedule between ages 62 and 67.

There is a long and short to the above. It is that, no matter how employer-sponsored plans may be sweetened or integrated, premature retirement is an unsatisfactory financial arrangement at best. It is even worse if one is terminated from employment before attaining age 55.

For our purposes, we regard any termination from employment under age $59^1/2$ — be it called layoff, downsizing, or early retirement — as being premature. Under this age, one is thrust into a whole new phase of livelihood activity for which he is often ill prepared. If he dares to dip into his meager retirement plan savings, he is hit with a 10% federal tax penalty (called: "additional tax") — PLUS, typically, a $2^1/2$% state tax penalty. These penalties [prescribed by IRC Sec. 72(t)(1)] plus the regular income tax on his drawdowns can deplete his retirement savings dangerously.

The message that we want to get across to you is this. If you are forced out of full-time employment before age $59^1/2$, take the best employer-sponsored retirement-plan package that you can. Then, immediately roll it over into an IRA account at the financial institution of your choice. DO NOT draw it down. That is, do not draw down any of the before-tax portion. The tax-free buildup and compounding over a pre-retirement period of 10 to 15 years can be quite dramatic. This is your best shot at preserving even a small nest egg for the future.

Commence a 3-IRA Plan

If your employment severance package consists of before-tax **and** after-tax portions, extra rollover precaution is required. You roll over only the before-tax portion into an IRA account. You need to deliberately separate out the after-tax portion: you've already paid tax on it. Use this portion for your living needs.

Being severed from employment in your early 50s can be an advantage . . . in a way. It will shock you out of any false sense of retirement security you might have had, and will force you to think about your future in more realistic terms. After numerous sleepless nights of worry, you'll come to the conclusion that you'll have to plan for your own retirement. You cannot rely on any employer nor can you rely on the government.

For facing this reality, we suggest you commence a 3-IRA plan. We depict such a plan in Figure 2.1. As so indicated, IRA #1 is a rollover account from all prior employer-sponsored plans from which you have been terminated. IRA #2 is a self-contributed deductible IRA, where IRA #3 is a self-contributed *nondeductible* IRA. A "deductible IRA" is when you get a tax deduction (adjustment to income) for your contributions, whereas you get no such deduction for a nondeductible IRA. Because different rules apply to rollover, deductible, and nondeductible IRAs, three separate accounts should be maintained.

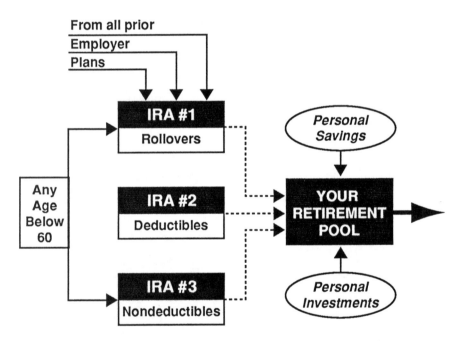

Fig. 2.1 - Use of 3-IRA Plan for Retirement "Make-Ups"

In 1987, several new twists were added to the IRA law (IRC Sec. 408). One twist was that if a worker is covered by a retirement plan of any kind, he could not get a full IRA deduction unless his modified AGI (Adjusted Gross Income) was $25,000 or less, if single, or $40,000 or less, if married. Between $25,000 and $35,000 (single), and between $40,000 and $50,000 (married), *partial* deductible IRAs were allowed. Beyond $35,000/$50,000, deductible IRAs were disallowed for active participants in employer plans.

Another twist was that *nondeductible* IRAs became popular with workers earning over $35,000/$50,000 who wanted to save additionally beyond their employer plans. Such IRAs, however, require the preparation of Form 8606: *Nondeductible IRAs (Contributions, Distributions, and Basis)*. The purpose of this form is to stake a claim in IRA #3 (in Figure 2.1) that tax already has been paid on your self-contributions. That is, Form 8606 establishes your **IRA basis** so that, when you draw the money out, you do not again pay tax on the contributory amounts. Meanwhile, the earnings in your nondeductible account ride along tax-deferred.

Apply for Unemployment Benefits

If you have been employed more or less regularly over the prior 25 years or so, you have built up a substantial *unemployment insurance* base in the state where you last worked. Although you did not contribute to the unemployment insurance fund yourself, your employer(s) did. All employers must pay insurance premiums into a State/Federal-sponsored unemployment benefits fund. As a consequence, each employee automatically has an insurance account with his appropriate state unemployment office.

For a person used to working 20 to 25 years or so, applying for unemployment insurance benefits can be a humiliating experience. Nevertheless, if you are dumped prematurely, we urge that you immediately apply for your benefits. No age requirement is involved (as it is with social security benefits). By "immediately," we mean the day, or day after, the termination notice from your employer becomes effective. Even then, there is a waiting period of several or more weeks, depending on the terms of your severance package.

The maximum unemployment benefits/compensation you can receive is approximately $200 per week. We say "approximately" because some states may pay a little higher (up to $230), while others may pay lower. It depends on the cost of living and insurance standards in each separate employment state. While $200 per week is not living high on the hog, this amount can at least help preserve your IRA accounts and other personal savings you might have.

The maximum continuous benefits period is 26 weeks. This is just six months. During this period, there is nearly $6,000 you can count on . . . while looking and searching for full- or part-time employment.

The irony is that any and all unemployment compensation you receive IS TAXABLE. Most states do not tax unemployment benefits, but the IRS always does [IRC Sec. 85(a)]. To be safe, figure that approximately 20% of your unemployment benefits will go to the IRS.

Another irony is that even though unemployment compensation is taxable as income, it does not qualify as "earnings" for contributions to your IRAs. The only earnings that qualify for IRAs are wages, salaries, bonuses, tips, commissions, and other amounts received for performing personal services. Thus, when collecting unemployment benefits, you have to seek compensation elsewhere in order to continue contributing to an IRA

Attend Resumé, Etc. Seminars

After registering with your nearest State Unemployment Office, ask them about any offerings of resumé seminars. Most unemployment offices either offer some instruction on preparing resumés or will put you in touch with professional resumé services. Or, one or two suitable reference books may be recommended to you. You simply must get a resumé of your background and experience updated and sharpened. While doing so, keep in mind that every prospective employer you contact will be receiving many hundreds of resumés for the same job opening you may be interested in. Therefore, you want to be able to prepare yours in a manner that stands out from the crowd. This requires study, effort, and ingenuity.

Also, while at the unemployment office, inquire about job-interview training classes. Some states offer these classes free; other states sponsor them through junior colleges and night schools for a small admissions fee. If necessary, get some private tutoring, but don't go overboard and spend too much for special tutoring. You don't want to become so overpolished that you appear insincere and disingenuous to a prospective employer.

Face it. Age and competition from others of your age are your vulnerable factors. While age discrimination is supposed to be against the law these days, it is still there. This is where ingenuity in your resumé comes in. One technique that might work is to state, on the front face of your resumé, your age. Accompany this with a recent photograph of yourself, dressed neatly. Engage a professional photographer. This way, because your age and photograph are displayed prominently, some prospective employers may "bend over backwards" to avoid your accusing them of age discrimination. By prominently displaying your age, you're almost daring them to turn you down on age alone.

Then focus your resumé on your career objectives and why your experience is unique towards that end. Be specific, but also be flexible. You have an agenda to complete and you can do it better than your competitors. By no means indicate or imply that your retirement goal has been cut short by premature severance from your prior employment. Employers do not care about your retirement goals; they only care about your knowledge and competence to make money for them.

As an overview of where you are at this stage of your life, we present Figure 2.2. This overview is a general roadmap of where you have been, and where you expect to go. You are not ready to retire at this point. You have much make-up work to do.

Apply to Temporary Hire Agencies

Being over age 50 and expecting to get a permanent full-time job with a new employer is unrealistic. Private employers have a "thing" about hiring individuals who are over 50. They are concerned about the extra cost of including such workers into their pension plans, health plans, and other fringe benefits that they

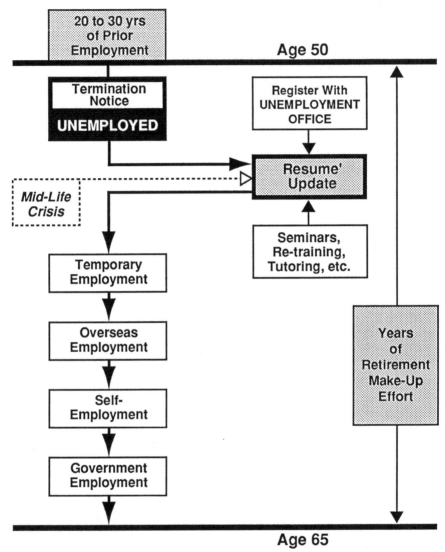

Fig. 2.2 - The Hurdles (and Agony) Ahead for Premature Retirees

provide to younger employees. Don't blame employers for this; blame the system. The "system" comprises all forms of *mandates* to employers by federal, state, and local governments. All mandates have a chilling effect on the willingness of employers to hire —

permanently — anyone over 50. This is a fact of premature retirement life.

The alternative is to seek temporary employment. The term "temporary" means less than one year with any particular employer. There are many temporary hiring agencies out there; apply to them. Look for job opportunity web sites on your Internet services. Surf the Web and look for temporary employment only. If you look for permanent employment and are lucky enough to get a few interviews, you'll just get more and more discouraged. So, set your sights on temporary employment, expecting to land between five and ten of these opportunities throughout your remaining working years. With the modern corporate fascination with downsizing — and, in some cases, overdownsizing — a new industry of temporary hiring is on the rise. Adjust to this new trend and make it work to your retirement advantage.

While temporarily employed and earning more than $2,000 in a given year, you can at least make contributions to an IRA. Whether it is deductible or nondeductible depends on your total gross income for the year, and on whether or not your spouse (if any, and if working) is an active participant in an employer-sponsored pension plan.

Do not begrudge and bemoan temporary employment. It has some advantages over permanent employment. For example, the hourly rate of pay is often higher. This is because the employer is spared some of the various mandates and does not have to offer any fringe benefits. Temporary hires are usually taken on during peak loads. Thus, an employer is willing to pay a little extra premium for qualified workers of his choice. You may work part time, full time, or overtime for temporary periods. If so, take advantage of the opportunity to earn extra money to put towards your own retirement.

In some cases, temporary employers (and, sometimes, the employment agencies themselves) permit participation in 401(k) deferred compensation or 408(k) simplified employee plans. This is particularly possible where all contributions are made by the employee: none by the employer. The 401(k) plans permit maximum contribution up to about $8,000 whereas the 408(k) plans permit up to about $15,000. Other than an additional small administration fee, these plans cost the employer nothing. Where offered, to temporary employees, these 401(k) and 408(k) plans generate much goodwill in the industry. Each time this opportunity presents itself, maximize your contributions for the year. When each temporary employment ends, roll your contributions over into your IRA #1 account in Figure 2.1.

Seek Overseas Employment

If your domestic temporary employments do not provide employer-sponsored participatory opportunities that exceed the $2,000 max IRA contribution, you should try other options. One such option is to seek employment overseas.

Many temporary hire agencies have international affiliates for placing U.S. workers in foreign countries. If not, try contacting the United Nations Employment Office in New York. Or, run a Positions Wanted ad on one or more web sites that service multinational corporations and business centers overseas. Skill in a foreign language, though helpful, is not always necessary. The English language is rapidly becoming the international language of business, largely through Internet communications.

Persons over age 50 are almost ideally suited for temporary employment overseas. Their children, if any, are grown and on their own. Persons over 50 probably have had some experience at traveling abroad. They are mature in their dealings with other nationals. They are usually married and are not expected to stay overseas and retire there indefinitely. They have a home in the U.S. and want to return to it.

Why are we suggesting temporary employment overseas?

Answer: There is a tax exemption bonanza of up to $70,000 per year at stake. This is a flat-out exclusion of this amount of income earned for personal services performed abroad. This is so prescribed by tax code Section 911: *Citizens or Residents of the U.S. Living Abroad.* The term "living abroad" means living on foreign soil for more than 330 days in any period of 12 consecutive months. Once this minimum 330-day period is attained, living abroad longer also qualifies (proportionately) for the "up to" $70,000 exclusion.

Section 911(b)(2) specifically states that—

The foreign earned income of an individual which may be **excluded** *under subsection (a)(1) for any taxable year shall not exceed the amount of foreign earned income* **computed on a daily basis** *at an annual rate of $70,000.* [Emphasis added.]

The term "an individual" is one worker performing personal service for which compensation is paid. Thus, a husband and wife, each separately working abroad, **each** could earn up to $70,000 and get **two** foreign earned income exemptions. To do so, each spouse must file a separate **Form 2555:** *Foreign Earned Income Exclusion*, and attach the two forms to their joint Form 1040. Working abroad and getting an income exclusion does not relieve a U.S. citizen or resident of filing annually his/her/their regular Form 1040 returns. By filing said returns, you have documentation as to where your tax exempt money came from.

The filing of Form 2555 can save an individual worker up to approximately $20,000 in federal taxes (if he earns up to $70,000 per year overseas). This $20,000 saving should be stuffed away to boost your retirement nest egg. You do this through a low-cost mutual fund that we made reference to back in Chapter 1. This money is after-tax money: the filing of Form 2555 makes it so. Thus, there is no need to worry about whether it fits into a tax-deferred retirement plan or not. Treat it as your personal retirement plan which you add to as opportunities arise.

Try Being Self-Employed

After working a few assignments as a temporary employee (domestic or foreign), it may dawn on you that you could do just as well hiring yourself out on your own. Whatever your training and experience have been, by the time you are 50-plus years old, you surely have acquired some expertise which can be marketed. If so, check local authorities for any licensing requirements, select yourself a fictitious business name, and set up an office or shop in your home to do business on your own. Then start advertising the availability of your services through community bulletin boards, classified ads in local news media, computer E-mail bulletins, and direct Internet solicitations to prospective customers and clients.

The idea is to "test the waters" on your own. Spend frugally and go visit prospective customers/clients on your own. Do everything possible to generate some income as an *independent contractor* to others. Whether you can generate enough income to support your customary living standards is another matter. You won't know until you at least give it a try. Try being self-employed for two to three years before giving up. You just don't know what the opportunities are, unless you go out and explore them on your own.

Above all, do not spend your savings to buy a franchise for some new product or service. All franchises require a large downpayment, "production quota" strings, and limit you to selling only the franchiser's product(s) or service(s). This pulls money out of your meager retirement funds which you can't afford. Nor can you afford to buy an existing business from a nonfranchisor.

Should your self-employment generate more than $10,000 net in a given year, new retirement savings opportunities open up. You can set up your own retirement plan historically known as a "Keogh Plan". Such a plan is now known as a 401(c) plan, or, more simply, as a *single participant* plan. It allows you to set aside up to 20% of your net earnings from self-employment for your own retirement. You may have a pension plan, a profit-sharing plan, or a combination of both. The key difference is that pension plans require fixed contributions each year, whereas profit-sharing plans do not.

To qualify for a Keogh plan, you must be self-engaged in a trade, business, or profession, and have positive net earnings from it. You need to have filed a Schedule C (1040): Profit or Loss from Business, a Schedule F (1040): Profit or Loss from Farming (or Fishing), **or** a Schedule K-1 (1065): Partner's Share of Income. Theoretically, you could contribute up to $30,000 into a Keogh plan each year. Expecting to do so is unrealistic unless your net earnings from self-employment exceed $150,000.

There's one major catch to self-employment retirement plans. If you have employees, you must include them in the plan and pay their contributions thereto. This reduces your net earnings which, in turn, reduces the contributions to your own plan. Since our focus here is on your own retirement, and since you are already over 50, we see no reason to take on any employees. If you need extra help, engage others who themselves are either independent contractors or who have separate businesses of their own.

Seek Government Employment

If self-employment is not for you, and temporary employment with private companies has turned you off, seek government employment. Government bodies at all levels (district, city, county, state, federal) have a good record as "equal opportunity" employers. Age, sex, race, or national origin are not detriments to employment. The fact that you may be over age 50 is not particularly a disadvantage. If you have the experience for a particular job opening, you have as much chance as a younger person.

Nearly one out of five employed persons in the nation are employed by some branch of government. In general, government bodies do not hire temporary workers. When a large segment of temporary work is necessary, it is contracted out to private companies. Other than a probationary period of six to 12 months, any hiring-on by a government agency tends to be permanent. However, the term "permanent" does not mean forever. It simply means that, when a worker is taken on, there is no preset termination date.

One of the — perhaps, THE — most attractive features of government employment is its income, retirement, and health care security. For those whose retirement prospects are otherwise grim, the security of government employment can be a comforting and productive experience. Especially for those who can weather the boredom and quagmires that government positions often entail. It is for this very reason that government retirement plans are a notch above those offered by private industry.

Most government bodies with open positions do not generally advertise them through private employment firms. Said positions are often listed with State Unemployment Offices, or are kept on hold until someone walks in. There is always a steady stream of job applicants to government agencies. You have to figure out your own way of discovering what positions are open.

Delay Sale of Residence

If none of the above re-employment efforts works out, do not panic and sell your home prematurely. Many persons who have been severed from employment prior to normal retirement likely have been working between 20 and 30 years. Over this period, they have sold and "rolled over" their capital gains from probably three to five residences. If so, they have built up quite an equity in their personal residence. Here, the term "equity" means market value less mortgage debt and selling expenses.

To illustrate what we are getting at, let us assume that, over your pre-retirement years of home ownership, you have built up an equity of $150,000 (possibly more). To a premature retiree, this amount could appear as a nest egg in and of itself. Thus, the temptation might be to sell your home, move to a less expensive area, and wait things out until social security kicks in. While waiting, the home equity nest egg is tapped into and consumed.

Our advice is: DO NOT sell your home prematurely. Instead, delay the sale as long as you can. Your equity is pretty safe where it already is. If economic pressures get too much for you, wait at least until you (or your spouse) is past age 55. There's a very worthwhile tax bonus if you do so.

Over-age-55 persons who sell their home get a $125,000 once-in-a-lifetime exclusion from any capital gain derived from the sale [IRC Sec. 121(b)]. For federal tax purposes, this converts into about $35,000 in tax savings. Add another $10,000 for state tax savings. Most states follow federal tax law on this over-55 home sale exclusion.

In summary, if you sell your home before attaining age 55 and have $150,000 or so of equity and capital gain in it, you stand to lose approximately $50,000 in federal/state income taxes alone. This $50,000 can go towards your own retirement support, rather than going to the government to support others. When forced onto the job market in your 50s, survival in retirement is your first priority.

To emphasize this point, we present Figure 2.3. As indicated therein, even if you sell one day after age 55, you still have seven

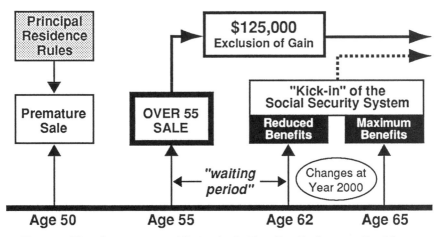

Fig. 2.3 - Time Importance of Delay in Selling Pre-Retirement Residence

years before social security kicks in (at age 62). Will the actual equity in your home support you for this length of time?

Tap Into Your Inheritance

Persons in their 50s have parents (if living) who are in their mid-70s and beyond. By this age, all parents have to prepare for passing their money and property onto their children and others. Much depends, of course, on the extent of accumulation and preservation of wealth by one's parents.

Financial actuaries have estimated that between 1990 and the year 2000, about 1 trillion dollars ($1,000,000,000,000) will pass to children from their parents. This averages about 100 billion dollars ($100,000,000,000) per year. From year 2000 to 2015, the average annual transfer of wealth through inheritance will exceed $300 billion. This is all the result of the cold-war-induced "inflationary bubble" in the 1960s, 70s, and 80s. Even modestly well off parents have experienced substantial appreciation in their property values and equity investments during this bubble period. All of this wealth becomes a potential *inheritance pool* for needy pre-retirees.

Tapping into one's inheritance before his parents decease is a very delicate matter. If handled crudely, there can arise sinister implications of depriving elderly parents of their right to enjoy their twilight years in peace. Therefore, before you can tap into your potential inheritance with a clear conscience, you must estimate the "worst case" needs of your elderly parents.

The **worst-case** parental need is full care in a nursing home for up to 10 years. In the majority of cases, full-care nursing rarely lasts more than three to five years. Nevertheless, the cost of full-care nursing home services ranges, nationwide, between $3,000 and $5,000 *per month*. This is around $50,000 per year. Thus, each living parent (in their mid-70s plus) will need approximately $500,000 (one-half million) to sustain life . . . to the very end. Consequently, if each of your parents has more than this amount accumulated from his life's work, investments, and savings, we urge that you approach them — delicately and sensitively. There's money there that legitimately will be yours some day, BUT you have a need for it now.

Once your parents' worst-case needs are provided for, they are in a position, financially, to help you with your premature retirement needs. For starters, each parent could give you outright a $10,000 cash gift each year, with no tax consequences to you. This amount is treated as after-tax dollars. Furthermore, each parent's $10,000 living gift to you will save that parent about $3,500 in federal/state transfer taxes . . . after his/her death. This is another case where it is better that you have the money rather than the government.

If each of your parents can afford to give you more than $10,000 in any given year, by all means accept it. Actually, each donor parent can cumulatively gift up to $600,000 without any direct tax consequences. However, from this point on, every dollar left in a parent's estate will be taxed at rates starting at 37% and going up to 55% for taxable estates over $3,000,000 (3 million). If you have parents who fall in this category, you could be doing them a favor by helping them to consume some of their money before they decease.

3

SELF-EMPLOYED PERSONS

A Self-Employed Individual Is Both An EmployER And An EmployEE. As such, You Can Establish A Qualified Plan For Yourself Either As A Keogh 401(c) Or A SEP/IRA 408(k). If You Do So, You Must Include All Other Employees. You Can Contribute Up To 25% Of Each Employee's Compensation (20% Of Yours) To A Keogh Plan, OR 15% (13.043% Of Yours) To A SEP/IRA. Having Any Employees Puts A "Damper" On Building Up A Sizeable Before-Tax Retirement Account For Yourself. Therefore, You Must Also Set Up Separately An AFTER-TAX Savings Plan . . . To Supplement Your Keogh Or SEP/IRA.

Self-employed persons are those who own their own business in proprietorship or partnership form. They are individuals who have started their businesses in one manner or another, and who stay with it to the end. The "end" being their own retirement. The event is usually signified by winding the business down, selling it to others, or transferring it to heirs.

Retirement from self-employment is the optimal form of voluntarism. One can retire early (in his 50s), normally (in his 60s), or late (in his 70s). There is no one standing ready to push said persons out the door. Nature may plan a role (through sickness, injury, or disability), but little else does. A self-employed person picks his own time and arrangement for retirement. Often, this is a slow and gradual transition process.

If you are self-employed, retirementwise you are one of the lucky few. You are lucky because — chances are — you've built up a comfortable nest egg in your 401(c) and 408(k) plans . . . plus your own personal savings and investments. Much, of course, depends on how long you have been self-employed: the longer the better. One of the distinguishing characteristics of self-employed individuals is the self-discipline to save and prepare for their own retirement without depending on the government. Financial security on one's own is perhaps the greatest reward of self-employment, particularly if your business has been at least modestly successful.

"Net Earnings" Explained

A self-employed person is both an employ**er** and an employ**ee**. As an employer, he can set up one or more employee retirement plans similar to any corporation. He can employ himself and others. As an employee, contributions can be made on his behalf to his employer-sponsored plans like any other employee. But there's a difference. His contributions are based on the *net earnings* of his business and not on any gross wages or salaries, as in the case of nonowner employees. In some years, the wages and salaries paid to other employees can exceed the owner's net earnings.

The term "net earnings from self-employment" is defined in Section 1402(a) of the tax code. The definition applies to proprietorships and partnerships only. It does not apply to corporations. In a corporation, all workers must be paid wages or salaries whether they are owners, part-owners, nonowners or not. The term "earnings" means the compensation that arises from the **personal services** of the proprietor or partner. These services must be more than incidental; they must be continuous and necessary day to day, to keep the trade, business, or profession alive.

In the case of a proprietorship, one individual owns the business 100%. In retirement plan terminology, he is called an "owner-employee." In the case of a partnership, an owner-employee is a partner who owns either more than 10% of the capital interest, or more than 10% of the profits interest, of the partnership. This 10% ownership threshold is designed to limit retirement plan contributions to active members of a general partnership.

Section 1402(a) goes on to define "net earnings" as—

- For proprietorships
  *— the gross income derived by an individual from any trade or business carried on by such individual, **less the deductions allowed** . . . which are attributable to such trade or business.* [Emphasis added.]

- For partnerships
  — the distributive share (whether or not distributed) of income or loss . . . from any trade or business carried on by a partnership of which [the individual] *is a member; except that in computing such gross income and deductions . . . there shall be excluded* [rental, interest, and dividend income, as well as capital gains or losses.]

Among the "deductions allowed" when computing net earnings from self-employment are:

(1) wages and salaries paid to nonowner employees,
(2) employer's 50% portion of the social security and medicare tax paid on behalf of nonowner employees,
(3) employer's contributions to retirement plans on behalf of nonowner employees.

Thus, one can readily sense that unless an owner's business is large enough and successful enough, his net earnings from self-employment are reduced substantially by the payouts to and for his nonowner employees. As a result, it is not uncommon for owners of proprietorships and partnerships to be placed in a position where contributions to their own retirement plans are less in amount than those of their nonowner employees.

Delay Plan Setups 3 Years

If you are, or expect to be, self-employed for 10, 20, or more years, it is difficult to see how you can operate successfully without ever engaging nonowner employees. It can be done with independent contractors, but it is difficult (we'll explain later). Once you have an employee other than yourself, you must include that employee and all others in any and all pension and profit-sharing plans that you may establish. You must do so under the *Minimum Participation Standards* set forth in Section 410 of the Internal Revenue Code.

The maximum participation delay that you can impose on an employee is two years of service [Subsec. 410(a)(1)(B)(i)]. For this delay, a "year of service" is a 12-month period during which an employee has performed not less than 1,000 hours of work. Typically, there are about 2,000 hours of full-time work in a normal 40-hour week, 50-week year (discounting two weeks for vacation). Thus, conceivably, it is possible to show a nonowner's work schedule to be less than 1,000 hours each year . . . for many years. Such skewing can be perceived as a discriminatory practice (especially if you pursue a consistent pattern in doing so). Unless based on bona fide business and economic reasons, any discriminatory pattern could result in disqualifying an otherwise tax-qualified retirement plan. When a before-tax retirement plan is disqualified, taxes on all current and prior contributions are imposed. Penalties and interest are then added.

Because of the possibility of disqualification for discriminatory practices, we urge that you not set up a retirement plan for your self-employment activities until you've been in such business for three or more years. If you can show from your tax filings that you did not set up a retirement plan for yourself until several years after you started business, it is not unreasonable nor discriminatory to hold your nonowner employees to the same standard. A 3-year delay is reasonable and makes practical sense. Few startups of self-employment businesses have contributory funds available in the first few years of operation.

It is not until one is in self-business on a *regular basis* that formal retirement plans should be considered. The "regular basis" concept arises from Section 1402(h) of the Code. This section states that—

An individual shall be deemed to be self-employed on a regular basis in a taxable year, or to be a member of a partnership on a *regular basis in such year, if he had net earnings . . . of not less than $400 in at least **two of the three consecutive taxable years immediately preceding** such taxable year from trades or businesses carried on by such individual or such partnership.* [Emphasis added.]

Here's an important point to keep in mind about self-employed retirement plans. There could be one or more taxable years in which there is a net earnings *loss*. In such event, as owner-employee you can make no contributions towards your own retirement. Yet, if you have nonowner employees, and had a formal *pension* plan for them, you'd be required to make contributions on their behalf. This is something you should think about.

Requirements for Qualification

Whether you are self-employed or employed by a corporation, the rules for tax qualifying a retirement plan are the same. These rules are set forth in complicated detail in Section 401: *Qualified Pension, Profit-Sharing, and Stock Bonus Plans.* This one section alone consists of approximately 16,000 statutory words. In addition, there are over 260,000 words of existing regulations, proposed regulations, court rulings, and IRS interpretations of what Section 401 means. Obviously, we can only scratch the surface of this complicated piece of retirement-plan legislation.

The basic requirements for qualification are prescribed in Section 401(a). Some 30 separate paragraphs of requirements are involved! The leadoff sentence to these 30 requirements reads—

*A trust created or organized in the United States and forming part of a stock bonus, pension, or profit-sharing plan of an employer for the **exclusive benefit of** his **employees** or their beneficiaries shall constitute a qualified trust under this section . . . if—* [Emphasis added.]

(2) under the trust instrument it is impossible . . . for any part of the corpus or income to be (within the taxable year or

thereafter) used for, or diverted to, purposes other than for the exclusive benefit of his employees or their beneficiaries;

(3) the plan . . . satisfies the requirements of section 410 (relating to minimum participation standards);

(4) the contributions or benefits provided under the plan do not discriminate in favor of highly compensated employees;

(13) the benefits provided under the plan may not be assigned or alienated;

(17) the annual compensation of each employee taken into account under the plan for any year does not exceed $150,000;

(26) on each day of the plan year [it] benefits . . . 40 percent or more of all employees of the employer;

. . . and so on.

In short, a qualified retirement plan is an **employees trust** where the employer's contributions are deductible from his gross income, and are exempt from tax to his employees . . . while in the trust. Tax does not apply until an employee or his beneficiary accepts one or more distributions from the trust. The general concept involved is presented in Figure 3.1. The trust assets are managed and invested by a third party custodian/trustee.

Master & Prototype Plans

There are many complications when setting up a retirement plan from scratch. This is because the rules have changed consistently every few years since 1962. Because of these frequent changes, the IRS has allowed regulated financial institutions to establish master and prototype plans which the institutions can offer to small businesses, whether in proprietorship, partnership, or corporate form. For owner-employees, these master/prototype plans are pitched as "Qualified *Keogh* Retirement Plans." The term "Keogh"

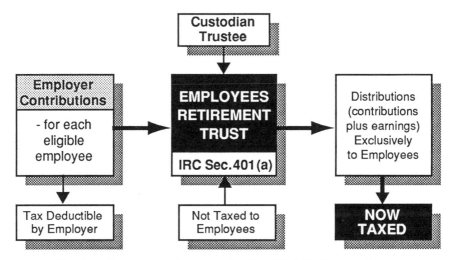

Fig. 3.1 - Conceptual Aspects of a Qualified Retirement Trust

is the name of the Congressman who sponsored the Self-Employed Individuals Tax Retirement Act of 1962. Keogh plans are now known as **Section 401(c) Plans**. This section of the tax code is now titled: Rules Relating to Self-Employed Individuals and Owner-Employees.

Typically, an owner-employee goes to the financial institution of his choice (bank, mutual fund, insurance company), and requests the appropriate application forms. These will be preprinted forms by the institution and will include:

1. Plan Adoption Agreement
   — for the owner-employer
2. Plan Enrollment Form
   — for each participating employee
3. One-Time Setup Fee
   — usually $50 to $100
4. Contributions Transmittal Form
   — for current year funding at setup
5. Transfer Authorization Form
   — for rolling over prior plan assets
6. Investment Option Form
   — for directing the type of investments

Each of these forms is a one-page contractual document of its own. It is quite simple and straightforward.

By far the most significant of the above listed forms is the Plan Adoption Agreement. The top portion lists essential information about the business; the mid portion states the participation requirements for employees, the percentage contribution of each, and other necessary information; the bottom portion is the signature authorization of the employer and the financial institution. A digest of the contents of this form is presented in Figure 3.2.

A separate set of the six documents above is required for each retirement plan established. For self-employers, the most common 401(c) plans are a Pension Plan *and/or* a Profit-Sharing Plan. A pension plan requires a fixed contribution each year, whereas a profit-sharing plan permits a variable contribution each year. Both are generically characterized as "defined contribution" plans.

Defined Contribution Plans

A defined contribution to a pension or profit-sharing plan is a *fixed percentage* of each participant's compensation for the year. For nonowner-employees, the compensation base is the gross amount shown in Box 1 of Form W-2: Wages, Tips, & Other Compensation. For owner-employees (self-employeds), the amount of compensation is the net earnings from the business after a certain "quirk adjustment" for the owner's self-employment tax

As for any tax benefit, there are certain limitations for defined contribution plans. These limitations — there are two — are set forth in Section 415(c)(1). This section prescribes that the amount of "annual addition" to a qualified plan cannot exceed—

. . . the lesser of—
(A) $30,000 or
(B) 25 percent of the participant's compensation

When two or more defined contribution plans are adopted, such as a Pension Plan **and** a Profit-Sharing Plan, they are treated as one plan for purposes of the contributory limitations above [Sec. 415(f)(1)(B)]. Thus, for example, there could be a 10% pension

---

ADOPTION AGREEMENT WITH ___*(Financial Institution)*___
for ☐ PENSION PLAN ☐ PROFIT SHARING PLAN

Business Information	Nature of Business _____

Name _____
Address _____
Phone _____
Employer Tax I.D. _____
Effective date of
this plan _____

Type: _____
☐ Proprietorship ☐ Partnership
☐ Corporation
This is:
☐ Initial Adoption ☐ Amended
No. of Employees _____

Elective Provisions

A. Participation shall not start before age _____
B. Years of service before participant eligible:
   ■ Immediate ■ 1 Year ■ 2 Years
C. Employer's contribution is [%] of the compensation of each
   participant each year.

Statutory Information

- Other related plans
- Notification of amendments
- Rollover of other assets
- IRS opinion letters
- MASTER/PROTOTYPE BASIC PLAN DOCUMENT

Authorization   Date signed _____

/s/ _____*(Authorized signature for business)*_____
/s/ _____*(Prototype agent's signature)*_____

Fig. 3.2 - Format/Contents of Prototype Keogh Plan: 401(c)

plan and a 15% profit-sharing plan. The two combined equal the 25% limitation above. The maximum 25% figure, however, applies only to nonowner-employees. Because of a computational quirk, a lesser percentage figure applies to owner-employees: those who get the business up and running.

All persons deriving net earnings from self-employment of $400 or more must pay a *self-employment tax*. This tax is a flat 15.3% rate; it is **in addition to** one's regular income tax rate.

Because a self-employed person is both an employer and employee, he is allowed to adjust his net profit from the business (for self-employment tax purposes only) by one-half of the 15.3% (which is 7.65%). Thus, his net earnings for self-employment tax purposes are his net profit times 92.35% (100% − 7.65% = 92.35%).

The net effect is that this special adjustment actually reduces an owner-employee's percentage contribution to his own plan. This has all been worked out into a conversion formula, which is:

$$\text{Converted \%} = \frac{\text{Selected \%}}{1 + \text{Selected \%}}$$

Here, the term "Selected %" is that which is selected (up to a maximum of 25%) for nonowner-employees. The "Converted %" is the corresponding equivalent for owner-employees.

For example, a selected % of 15% converts to 13.043% as follows:

$$\text{Converted \%} = \frac{15\%}{1 + 15\%} = \frac{15\%}{115\%} = 13.043\%$$

Similarly, a selected % of 25% (the maximum) converts to 20% for an owner-employee.

Thus, while an employee's compensation could be multiplied by 25% to compute his plan contributions, a self-employed's net profit would be multiplied by 20% to compute his defined contributions.

Ways to Avoid Employees

There is no question about it. If self-employed persons could avoid employees altogether, they could amass quite substantial amounts in their qualified retirement plans. Especially so if such plans were funded over a period of 10, 20, or more years. The obvious reason is that there would be no dilution of contributory money for employees.

How does one go about avoiding employees by a proprietorship or partnership over a long period of time?

There are several approaches, but none is guaranteed to work for more than a few years. One could farm out all work to others who are in business for themselves. One could engage independent contractors on a job-by-job basis. One could contract with a temporary hire agency to supply part-time workers. One could lease employees from an employment leasing agency.

The problem with all of these approaches is that you run into the *leased employee rule* of Section 414(n). This is a 1,200-word rule, the essence of which is—

If—
*(A)   services are provided pursuant to an **agreement** between the recipient and any other person,*
*(B)   such person has performed such services for the recipient . . . on a **substantially full-time** basis for a period of at least 1 year, and*
*(C)   such services are of a type **historically performed**, in the business field of the recipient, by **employees*** [then]—

. . . [that person] *shall be treated as an employee of the recipient.* [Emphasis added.]

So, no matter what you try to do, the IRS, U.S. Dept. of Labor, State Employment Agencies, and Health Security Enforcers will always attempt to classify your workers as employees rather than as nonemployees.

BUT, if you can "historically structure" your business in a bona fide way that necessitates the engagement of **independent contractors**, you have a good chance of succeeding without employees. For example, you can engage a telephone answering service to take your phone messages and make your appointments. You can engage a secretarial service to type your letters and type your reports. You can engage free-lance writers, artists, consultants, technicians, handymen, and the like. You can engage — and re-engage as necessary — one or more subcontractors to do a specific job or phase of a specific job. There are some 80 different work occupations which have been held to be independent contractors (nonemployees) by various judicial and IRS rulings. The point is that in a "free society," you can engage and disengage whomever whenever you want. That is, until the IRS comes along and starts dictating to you its theory about "common law" employees. Your only defense is a showing that you have maintained strictly a nonemployee posture at all times.

You have to be able to show that the day-to-day chores of the business are run by you and your spouse (if any). Then you have to make sure that each worker, agency, vendor, or subcontractor that you engage submits to you an *invoice statement* for each billing period that services are rendered. See to it that the billing periods are irregular, and that they are directly related to specific work accomplishment. Other practical tips for maintaining your nonemployees are presented in Figure 3.3. The whole idea is that each nonemployee is in a separate business of his own. He funds his own retirement plan(s), if any, separate and apart from yours.

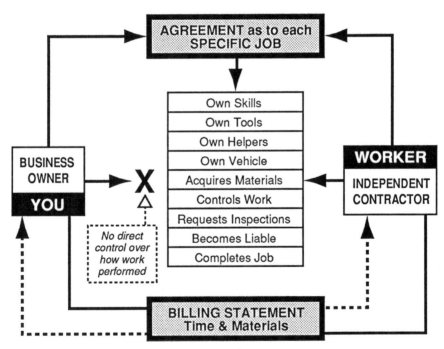

Fig. 3.3 - Precautions for Maintaining Nonemployee Status of Workers

SEP/IRA: 408(k) Plans

In a proprietorship or partnership lasting 10 to 20 years or more, it may be impractical to maintain a strict nonemployee posture at all times. Sooner or later, the business will need a few regular employees. If for no other reason, a handful of reliable nonowner-employees is needed to maintain continuity of policy in business transactions and continuity of quality of products and services. Consequently, many small businesses have found that a formula for success is a combination of engaging employees and nonemployees. The employees are included in the business owner's retirement plan(s) whereas the nonemployees are not.

A simple retirement plan where only a handful (less than 25) of employees is involved is a SEP/IRA or a Section 408(k) plan. The acronym SEP stands for *Simplified Employee Pension*, and is the title of Section 408(k). This section requires that all workers who are paid at least $300 for services performed in each of at least three years in a consecutive 5-year period must be included in the business owner's retirement plan. A SEP combines the ease of administration of an IRA with most of the benefits of Keogh 401(c) plans. Master/prototype adoption agreements are also available for SEP/IRAs.

The idea behind a SEP plan is that each eligible employee sets up his/her own IRA account with a financial institution of his/her own choice. Once the employee does this, the employer is obliged to make profit-sharing-type contributions. These contributions must be at least 3% of each employee's annual compensation [Sec. 416(c)(2)(A)]. The maximum contributions are limited to the *lesser of* $30,000 or 15% (13.043% for the owner-employee) of each participating employee's compensation.

ALL eligible employees must set up their own individual SEP/IRA accounts. If any eligible employee objects to setting up an IRA, the SEP arrangement is disqualified for all. Rather than allowing one employee to disqualify a SEP/IRA arrangement for all, that employee can be terminated for "good cause."

Once a SEP contribution is made on behalf of a nonowner-employee, it is 100% vested in that employee. Thereafter, each participant can direct his investments any way he wants; can make withdrawals; can make rollovers from other IRA or other pension accounts; can make separate IRA contributions of his own (under the regular IRA rules); and can transfer his account to any authorized SEP/IRA trustee at any time. This way, the employer-contributor is totally free of any aggregate accounting for — or safeguard of — employee funds.

An employer cannot set up a SEP plan if he currently maintains any other qualified plan. If he has a one- or two-plan Keogh in existence, for example, he has to terminate that plan. Doing so means that he has to distribute totally all plan assets proportionately to each Keogh participant. Once this is done, he can immediately commence a SEP plan. One nice advantage of the SEP is that the distributions from a terminated Keogh can be rolled over into each participant's SEP/IRA if he/she so chooses.

The "Differential Vesting" Game

The term "vesting" is tax defined as an employee's *nonforfeitable right* to a percentage of the employer's contribution to his retirement plan. A "vesting schedule" is a step-wise increase in the nonforfeitable percentage until 100% vesting is achieved on or before the employee attains normal retirement age. Vesting schedules are based on the number of years of service completed. In the early years of plan participation, the incremental increases in nonforfeitures traditionally have been smaller than the incremental increases in the later years. This made vesting rights disproportionate to the years of service, and skewed the employer contributions more towards forfeitures than nonforfeitures. Thus, the game of "differential vesting" arose. Employers devised schemes to terminate less productive employees before reaching their 50% vesting rights.

Prior to 1992, vesting schedules up to 15 years were allowed for Keogh-type plans. This provided opportunity for owners of a business — who knew they were going to stay with the business — to play the differential vesting-schedule game with their employees. If an employee did not reach 100% vesting when terminated, his nonvested portion of the employer's contributions were forfeited. The forfeited contributions remained in the plan to increase the potential benefits of those who attained normal retirement. The owners of a business were the obvious beneficiaries of these practices.

For years 1992 and later, all forfeitures of early-departing employees are treated as part of the annual addition to all participants in the plan. That is, each participant shares proportionately in all forfeitures at the end of each plan year. This sharing of forfeitures reduces the employer's contributions for that year. The general effect of this sharing of forfeitures is presented in Figure 3.4.

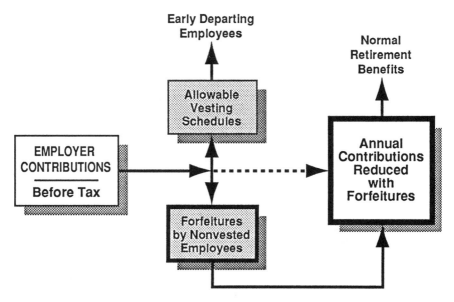

Fig. 3.4 - Forfeitures Now Part of Employer Contributions Annually

The "annual addition" is statutorily defined as—

... the sum for any year of—
(A) employer contributions,
(B) the employee contributions, and
(C) **forfeitures** [Sec. 415(c)(2)]. [Emphasis added.]

The annual additions per participant are limited, as previously explained under defined contribution plans.

As the rules now stand, if a proprietorship or partnership owner wants to adopt a Keogh-type plan, and wants to use a vesting schedule, he is limited to requiring a maximum eligibility waiting period of one year for his nonowner-employees [Sec. 410(a)(1)(A)(ii)]. He then can adopt a 5-year or 7-year vesting schedule [Sec. 411(a)(2)(A),(B)]. In the 5-year schedule, the nonforfeitable percentage is 20% each year, culminating in 100% vesting after completing the five years. In the 7-year schedule, zero % applies to the first two years. After the third and subsequent years, at 20% vesting each, 100% vesting is attained after completing the seven years.

The whole 1990s trend is towards accelerated 100% vesting for all employees: owners and nonowners alike. No vesting schedule is needed if a plan provides for 100% nonforfeitable rights immediately upon attaining eligibility for participation. In this case, employers can require a 2-year participation waiting period for Keogh-type plans or a 3-year period for SEP/IRA plans.

Importance of Supplemental Savings

During the 2-year or 3-year waiting periods above, no employer contributions are made on behalf of waiting employees. But the moment an employee becomes eligible to participate, any employer contributions to the retirement plan become 100% nonforfeitable by the employee. This means that for post-1991 years, owner-employees have nil opportunity to enhance their own nest egg with forfeitures of their employees.

As a result of the above, the trend in small businesses these days is the adoption of variable contribution profit-sharing plans of the Keogh or SEP/IRA types. Of these, SEP/IRA plans are definitely more advantageous. There is simplicity of setup and administration, with a 3-year waiting period. During this 3-year period, an owner-employee (provided he has been in business longer than three years) can contribute to his own SEP/IRA even though no contributions are made for his less than 3-year employees. This can give the owner-employee a head start on his newer employees. But there can be no enhancement through vesting forfeitures of his older employees.

So, how does a self-employed business owner build up a retirement nest egg that is more in keeping with his old-age goals?

Answer: He starts and contributes to his own **after-tax** retirement savings. By making his "supplemental plan" an after-tax contributory account, he is not obliged to make any contributions on behalf of his nonowner-employees. It is best to do this through one or more low-cost mutual funds.

There are many low-cost mutual funds available, as we discussed in the latter part of Chapter 1. The focal difference here is on tax-free municipal bond funds. If you start soon enough in your self-employment business, tax-free compounding of your investment earnings can be quite significant by the time you are ready to retire.

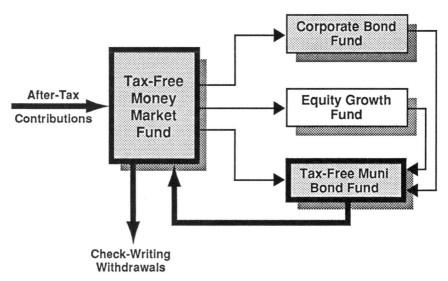

Fig. 3.5 - Supplemental Retirement "Plan" for Self-Employeds

As kind of a guideline, we suggest an arrangement along the lines depicted in Figure 3.5. Preferably, select a mutual fund management company which has been in business 10 years or more, which offers a "family of funds." This way, you can telephone-switch among the funds with great ease. The idea is to have one dominant tax-free fund as your compounding source for long-term buildup. Other taxable funds are used to provide enhanced yields as investment opportunities arise.

Be Aware of Form 5500-C/R

If you have a SEP/IRA, a profit-sharing Keogh, or a pension-type (money purchase) Keogh, you have no choice but to include your employees in those plans. This is because they are before-tax plans. As such, each plan requires the annual filing of Form 5500-C/R. The official title of this form is: **Return/Report of Employee Benefit Plan.** The letters "C/R" have no acronymic significance other than being intended for plans with fewer than 100 participants. This number of participants targets most self-employed businesses.

Form 5500-C/R consists of six pages comprising nearly 150 entries. The form is accompanied by 18 pages of instructions in 3-columnar text. Completing this form properly definitely requires professional assistance. Because of its complexity, its due date is *the last day of the 7th month after the plan year ends.* For calendar-year plans, this means July 31st.

At the top of the form, below the bold imprinted plan year, there is a statement which reads—

This Form is Open to Public Inspection

This means that each participant employee can have access to the form and its entry information.

Why would an employee want to see Form 5500-C/R?

Answer: Because on page 6 thereof, there is a summary-type financial statement listing the assets and liabilities of the plan, and its income and expenses for the year. Of particular interest to all participants is the expense entry labeled: *Distribution of benefits and payments to provide benefits.* This entry is most often questioned when the owner-employee commences drawing his own benefits from the plan.

4

PLAN DISTRIBUTION OPTIONS

Qualified (Tax Deferred) Retirement Plans Comprise The Gamut Of Pension, Profit-Sharing, Stock Bonus, Annuity, And Elective Deferral Arrangements. Generally, Distributions From These Plans Are Taxable Under Section 72 As Annuities. These Are Periodic Payments For A Term Of Years Certain, Single Life, Or Joint And Survivor Lives . . . At The Option Of Each Distributee. If Under Age 70^{1}/2, "Rollovers" Into Another Similar Plan Or Into An IRA Are Allowed. In Certain Cases, Lump-Sum Distributions May Qualify — Once In Your Lifetime — For Special Tax Treatment Called: The "5- or 10-Year Option."

The term "plan" as used in this chapter refers specifically to an *employer* sponsored retirement plan. Excluded are IRA plans, SEP/IRAs, and social security. These will be covered in subsequent chapters.

The term "employer" can be any kind of employer: large corporation, small corporation, partnership, proprietorship, government agency, school district, fire and police departments, religious and charitable organizations, collective bargaining, and so on. There may be — and often is — more than one plan offered by the same employer. In which case, in aggregate, they are considered as one plan. Each retirement plan may be one of five general types, namely: pension, profit-sharing, stock bonus, annuity, and elective deferral. Collectively, they are referred to as "pension and annuity" plans.

The term "distribution" means the withdrawal of money or property from a plan, and turning it over to one or more employee participants. For each participant, an individual account is maintained. The Tax ID (social security number) of each participant is used for account identification.

Distributions are required to be made whenever an employee is *separated from service*. An employee is "separated" from employment **only on** his death, retirement, resignation, or discharge. An employee who continues in the same job for a different employer as the result of liquidation, merger, consolidation, or reorganization of his former employer is not considered to be separated.

The sole and exclusive purpose of every retirement plan is to make distributions to its participants. A plan cannot go on and retain its assets forever. In this chapter, therefore, we want to focus on the distribution options that face every employee when he separates from service. Some of these options are easy choices, some are not. Does he pay tax now, pay it later, or pay it monthly over the rest of his life? Much depends on the tax status of the plan: before-tax or after-tax. Much also depends on the age of the employee, his financial status, state of health, and likelihood of re-employment. Making the best choice depends on all facts and circumstances that exist at the time of separation.

Where the Confusion Starts

All plan administrators are required to notify participants each year — and certainly upon separation — of the total value of each participant's plan account(s). This is done following the end of each plan year. If there are two or more plans by the same employer, they are either adopted simultaneously or amended so as to become simultaneous plan years.

Invariably, a plan year differs from that of an employer's fiscal year and from that of an employee's calendar year. The plan year differs because all plan assets — contributions, forfeitures, and earnings — are held in trust. A trust is an independent accounting entity from that of the employer or the employee. Its plan year may end on April 30, for example, while an employer's fiscal year may end on September 30 and an employee's calendar year ends December 31. These different ending dates can be a source of confusion when distributions are made. The year of concern to a distributee is that calendar year in which a plan administrator "closes his books" on the separating employee. The actual receipt of distributions from the closing-the-books year may not come until six months later, in a different calendar year for the employee.

While plan year identity is one source of confusion, the greatest source of confusion has to do with the type of trust from which the distributions are made. For tax identity purposes, there are two types of employee trusts. There are *exempt* trusts and *nonexempt* trusts. An exempt trust is an entity whose earnings qualify under Section 501(a) for exemption from all income taxation, until the trust assets are distributed. A nonexempt trust does not qualify under Section 501(a). Most employer-sponsored plans try to avoid nonexempt (disqualified) trusts.

Many distributees do not fully understand why the distinction between before-tax and after-tax components of their retirement accounts is so important. All before-tax distributions are taxable to the distributee, whereas after-tax distributions are nontaxable. They are "nontaxable" to the extent that tax already has been paid on the designated contributions . . . by the employee. If the distinction is not clear, a distributee winds up paying tax again on his nontaxable distributions.

For each exempt employee's trust, there are four sources of asset accumulations. These sources are—

- Employer's contributions (mostly before tax)
- Employee's contributions (before **and** after tax)
- Forfeitures (by nonvested separatees)
- Earnings (while in the trust)

Do keep in mind that these four contributory sources may accrue simultaneously in an exempt trust.

A well-designed distributee statement would clearly indicate the type of assets and their value, categorized as before tax and after tax. Later, you'll see that the after-tax component has an important bearing on establishing your "exclusion ratio," when receiving distributions in the form of annuity payments. The overall clarification that we have in mind is presented in Figure 4.1. Most plan administrators do not always make the before-tax/after-tax distinction clear. Therefore, it behooves you as a distributee to make specific clarifying inquiry to the administrator of each of your retirement plans.

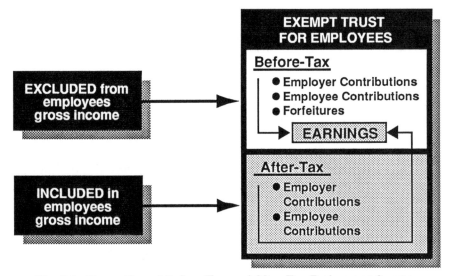

Fig. 4.1 - Separation of Before-Tax and After-Tax Retirement Assets

Distributions Taxable as Annuities

When distributions are made from a qualified employee's trust, Section 402 comes into play. This section is titled: *Taxability of Beneficiary of Employees' Trust*. This section — consisting of approximately 6,000 statutory words — is crucial to understanding the choices that distributees have when they retire or otherwise separate from service. But the choices are not always clear from statutory wording itself. You'll see this lack of clarity in Subsection 402(a) below.

Subsection 402(a) reads in full as follows:

Except as otherwise provided in this section, any amount actually distributed to any distributee by any employees' trust

*described in section 401(a) which is exempt from tax under section 501(a) **shall be taxable** to the distributee, in the taxable year of the distributee in which distributed, under section 72 (**relating to annuities**).* [Emphasis added.]

The gist of this section is that tax will be paid by the distributee in the same manner as tax is paid on an annuity. The characteristic of an annuity is that payments are made monthly. This is the normal way for receiving a retirement pension. Unfortunately, the monthly payments also include a portion of the after-tax contributions which an employee may have made. Thus, the question arises: How do the after-tax contributions avoid being taxed a second time? This is where knowing the principles of annuity taxation comes in.

Annuity taxation involves the computation of an **exclusion ratio.** It is in this exclusion ratio that the proportion of after-tax contributions to the total monthly payments is factored out. The result is a taxable portion and a nontaxable portion of each monthly payment. We'll tell you more about this process later.

In the meantime, back to Section 402(a). The statutory wording is such that the primary expectation is that distributions will be made monthly. But what if a distributee doesn't want his distributions monthly? This is where the opening phrase: *Except as otherwise provided in this section* comes into action. One has to plod through and study the other provisions of Section 402 to find out where the exceptions to monthly payments are.

There are 10 subsections to Section 402. Upon plodding through the 6,000 (or so) words thereof, we come to subsections (c) and (d) which allow alternatives to monthly distribution. These two subsections are titled:

402(c) — Rules Applicable to **Rollovers**
402(d) — Tax on **Lump Sum** Distributions

Thus, as emphasized in bold type, there are two alternatives to monthly payments: rollovers and lump sum distributions. A "rollover" postpones the tax until later, whereas a "lump sum" enables the distributee to pay the tax upfront . . . and be done with it. Let's review each of these options separately.

Rollover Option Requires Care

The word "rollover" has a lilting tone of simplicity to it. You just roll over your retirement plan balance from one account to another similar account, and that's it. But it is not this simple. There are certain rules, restrictions, and limitations that apply. Altogether, there are 10 such rules. The 10 are prescribed in the 1,500-word Section 402(c): Rules Applicable to Rollovers from Exempt Trusts.

The overall gist of Section 402(c) is that—

(1) If . . . (A) any portion of the balance to the credit of an employee in a qualified trust is paid to the employee in an eligible rollover distribution, . . . (B) the distributee transfers any portion of . . . such distribution to an eligible retirement plan, . . . then such distribution (to the extent transferred) shall not be includible in gross income for the taxable year in which paid. [Emphasis added.]

In other words, *any portion* of the distribution which is properly rolled over is excluded from the distributee's income for current (distributable year) taxation purposes. There is no requirement that the entire distributable amount be rolled over. The portion which is not rolled over is taxed currently. The portion which is rolled over will be taxed later when it is ultimately withdrawn from the rollover account. Thus, a rollover permits elective discretion as to what portion is taxed and what portion is not taxed, currently.

Most distributees understand that a rollover must be completed within 60 days of the receipt of the money or property distributed [Sec. 402(c)(3)]. This is pretty common knowledge these days. Also, most distributees know that the rollover amount must go into an eligible — meaning "tax qualified" — retirement account (such as an IRA) where it continues to earn income tax-free. These understandings hold true when a plan participant dies and his spouse receives the distribution. She, too, can exercise the rollover option as though the surviving spouse were the employee participant.

Where rollover problems arise, and where care is required, has to do with the meaning of "eligible" rollover distributions. This is that emphasized phrase in Section 402(c)(1) above. What does the term "eligible" actually mean?

The term "eligible" means several things. Firstly, it means that a rollover can only be made from exempt (before-tax) trusts. Secondly, the rollover amount must be stripped of any after-tax contributions that went into the exempt trust. This is the confusing part, as otherwise you pay a second time on money or property when subsequently distributed from the rollover account. Thirdly, to be eligible, the rollover amount must NOT be a "required distribution" caused by—

(a)   disqualification of a trust,
(b)   death of a participant where the proceeds go to other than spouse or children, or
(c)   distributee attaining age 70$^{1/2}$ or older.

And, fourthly, an eligible rollover is an amount which is NOT—

. . . one of a series of substantially equal periodic payments (not less frequently than annually) made—
(i) for the life (or life expectancy) of the employee or the joint lives (or joint life expectancies) of the employee and the employee's designated beneficiary, or
(ii) for a specified period of 10 years or more.
[Sec. 402(c)(4)(A).]

In other words, you cannot abort a regular annuity contract payout and divert it into a rollover account to defer tax on the annuity distribution.

For summary purposes, we present in Figure 4.2 the key essentials of an eligible rollover contribution. As you can sense from this figure, rollovers cannot be made blindly. The account holder (plan participant) must expressly instruct the relinquishing trustee to strip out the after-tax amounts and *not* report them (to the IRS) as taxable distributions.

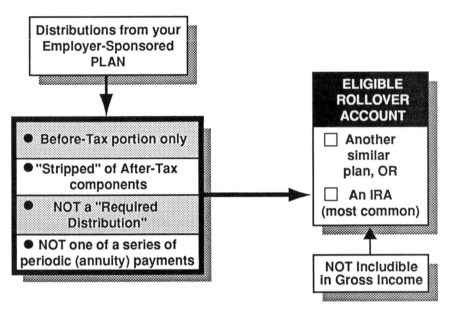

Fig. 4.2 - Requirements for an "Eligible" Rollover Distribution

Rollovers Other Than Money

An eligible rollover distribution can also include property other than money. In some employer plans, there is provision for participants to designate their investment preferences. These designations may be employer securities, mutual funds, real estate, collectibles, etc. Whatever the property form, it qualifies as an eligible distribution if the provisions of Figure 4.2 apply.

Whether the money or property is distributed, it is important always to keep one point in mind. If the distribution consists of any cumulative after-tax amount, said amount must be stripped off and handled separately. It is "return of capital" . . . which is not taxed a second time.

If the distributed property is sold and the proceeds — in whole or part — are rolled over, a special rule comes into play. This is subsection 402(c)(6)(A)–(D) titled: *Sales of Distributed Property*. Subrule (A) treats *any portion* of the sale proceeds that is rolled over as an eligible distribution. Subrule (B) treats the excess proceeds of the sale price over the property's fair market value at time of distribution also as an eligible distribution.

Subrule (D) states that—

No gain or loss shall be recognized on any sale described in subparagraph (A) to the extent that an amount equal to the proceeds is . . . [rolled over].

This is another way of saying that, since no tax has been paid on the eligible distribution, there is no "tax basis" in the property from which to establish a tax recognized gain or loss. For example, suppose the value of property when distributed is $60,000. Within 60 days, the distributee sells the property for $70,000 and rolls the entire amount into a qualified rollover account (such as an IRA). The $10,000 gain (at the time of the rollover) is not recognized as such and is, therefore, not includible in the gross income of the distributee. Similarly, had the property been sold for $50,000. The $10,000 loss would not be tax recognized.

Subrule (C) [of Sec. 402(c)(6)] gives the distributee the right to designate the constituents of the rollover. This right applies to those situations where the eligible distribution consists of money and property, and subsequently (within 60 days) the property is sold. If all the money and proceeds are not rolled over, the distributee can designate that portion of the aggregate which is to be treated as—

(i)   . . . attributable to amounts not included in gross income, and
(ii) . . . included in the rollover contribution.

We try to depict in Figure 4.3 this elective concept. You must make your designation decision when you file your tax return for the rollover year. Once you make your decision, it becomes irrevocable.

Required Explanation of Rollovers

Effective for distributions made after 1992, plan administrators are required to provide recipients of eligible rollover distributions

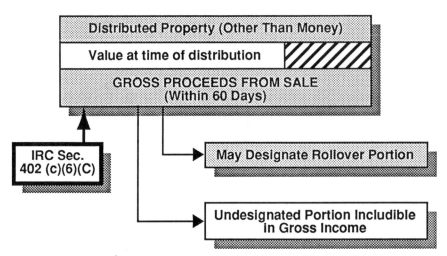

Fig. 4.3 - Election Option When Distributed Property is Sold (Within 60 Days)

with a written explanation of their decision-making rights. This is a statutory requirement set forth in Section 402(f): Written Explanation to Recipients . . . etc. The essence of this requirement is that you be put on notice that you are subject to a mandatory 20% withholding if you decide against a direct (trustee-to-trustee) rollover. The notice must be furnished to you not more than 90 days and not less than 30 days *before* the actual distribution. This is to allow you an extra 60 days' time to make up your mind.

This 60-day notice before distribution is one of those irritating contradictions of law imposed by the IRS. Statutorily, you are allowed 60 days *after* receipt of distributions to make your decision [Sec. 402(c)(3)]. Yet, through regulation, the IRS comes along and says that if any money or property passes through your hands, 20% of the distributed value is arbitrarily withheld as tax. So, even if you decide to roll over 100% of the proceeds, the IRS already has taken 20%. This means that you must find other money to replace the 20% arbitrarily withheld by the IRS. After replacement, you have to file for a refund of the 20%. This takes about 18 months.

To explain its action, the IRS has prepared **Notice 92-48**: *Special Tax Notice Regarding Plan Payments*. Its headnote summary reads in part—

A payment from the Plan that is eligible for "rollover" can be taken in two ways. You can have all or any portion of your payment either—
  (1) PAID IN A "DIRECT ROLLOVER" or,
  (2) PAID TO YOU.
. . . This choice will affect the tax you owe.

If you choose to have your Plan benefits PAID TO YOU:
  • You will receive only 80% of the payment, because the Plan administrator is required to withhold 20% of the payment and send it to the IRS as income tax withholding to be credited against your taxes.

This and other portions of IRS Notice 92-48 are paraphrased by the plan administrator, and passed on to each distributee. The administrator's explanation also includes a description of payments that cannot be rolled over (such as your after-tax contributions), and choices by surviving spouses, alternate payees (in connection with divorce or legal separation), and other beneficiaries (who cannot roll over). The required explanation also warns you that, if you are under age 59$1/2$, you are subject to an additional 10% tax on the portion that you do not roll over.

Lump-Sum Tax Treatment

The administrator's explanation required by Section 402(f) may also include other information. Specifically, if your distribution qualifies as a "lump sum," you may be eligible for special tax treatment called: *forward averaging.* To qualify as a lump sum, the payment must be made within one year. It must also include the *entire balance* in all related retirement plans of your employer. Furthermore, you must have been a participant in the plan for at least five years.

If your distribution qualifies, choosing lump-sum tax treatment is a way to pay all the tax currently . . . and be done with it. No rollovers of any kind are required, nor permitted. You pay the tax on the lump sum, and use the remainder of your distribution any way you see fit. You are no longer obligated to keep track of it as before-tax money or property.

The special averaging rules on lump-sum distributions are prescribed in Section 402(d): Tax on Lump-Sum Distributions. This section consists of approximately 1,800 words. Basically, it is a one-time election to use "5-year averaging" after attaining age 59 1/2. This forward-averaging method can result in significantly lower tax than would be the case if the same amount of distribution were included in gross income and taxed at your regular rates.

If you were born before January 1, 1936, two "grandfather" options apply. You can use 10-year averaging instead of 5-year averaging. The 10-year averaging process results in less tax than the 5-year method. In addition, if you have any pre-1974 participation in the plan, you may elect to have that portion flat taxed at a rate of 20%. And you can still use 10-year averaging on the balance.

A special rule applies when employer stock or securities are included in the lump-sum distribution [Sec. 402(d)(4)D)(ii)]. The rule is directed at the Net Unrealized Appreciation (NUA) of the employer's stock (if any) while held by the plan. The employer stock included in the payment must be attributable to your after-tax stock purchases contributed to the plan. For example, suppose that your employer's stock that you purchased with after-tax money and contributed to the plan was worth $1,000. When you received the stock from the plan, it was worth $1,200. You now have $200 of NUA. Under the special rule, you do not have to pay tax on the $200 until later when you sell the stock.

Form 4972: Lump-Sum Averaging

If you otherwise qualify, computing the amount of tax on your lump-sum distribution by the special 5-year averaging method is indeed advantageous. It is so for three reasons, namely:

1. The tax is computed separately from all other sources of income you may have in the distribution year. This is doable because the tax on the lump-sum amount is based on single person rates. Thus, it makes no difference what your regular filing status is.

2. If your total distribution is less than $70,000, you get a "minimum distribution allowance" not to exceed $10,000 (subject to phase-out).

3. The tax is figured on one-fifth or 20% of your "adjusted taxable amount," then multiplied by 5. For example, if your adjusted taxable amount is $75,000, the tax is figured on $15,000 ($75,000 ÷ 5) times 5. Because of rate differentials, the tax is lower on $15,000 times 5 (at 15%) than on $75,000 (at 30%).

To determine whether or not you can choose lump-sum averaging, you must review **Form 4972** AND its instructions. This form is titled: Tax on Lump-Sum Distributions. Immediately below this title is an instruction which says—

Use This Form Only for Lump-Sum Distributions from Qualified Retirement Plans. [Meaning only from private employer-sponsored pension, profit-sharing, or stock bonus plans. Distributions from IRAs, SEP/IRAs, tax-sheltered annuities, or federal employee plans do not qualify.]

Part I of Form 4972 is titled: ***Complete this part to see if you qualify to use Form 4972.*** This part of the form has a series of questions, each of which must be answered "Yes" or "No" in check-box fashion. These questions, edited and abbreviated for our purposes here, are presented in Figure 4.4. Each question has to be answered in the order listed, as you may be disqualified before you get to the last question.

The 5-year averaging process is a 22-step computational procedure. We'll not go into this computation here, as it is quite self-explanatory on Form 4972. If you qualify for use of the form, by all means use it. Taxwise, it is preferable to any other plan distribution option you have.

Three Annuity-Type Choices

If your distribution does not qualify for lump-sum averaging, or is not rolled over to an IRA or to another type of qualified plan, it is

Form 4972	Tax on Lump-Sum Distributions		Year	
Name of recipient of distribution		**Tax I.D.** _____		
Part I	**To See If You Qualify**		**Yes**	**No**
1	Did you roll over any part of the distribution? - If "yes", do not complete rest of form.	1		
2	Was this distribution the **entire balance** from a qualified pension, profit-sharing, or stock bonus plan? - If "no", do not complete rest of form.	2		
3	Were you in the plan for at least 5 years before this lump-sum distribution? - If "no", see instructions on official Form 4972	3		
4	Were you 59 1/2 or older at the time of the distribution? - If "no", do not complete rest of form.	4		
5	Were you an employee who received the distribution because of separation from service? - If "no", see instructions on official Form 4972	5		
6	Did you use Form 4972 in a prior year for any distribution received after 1986? - If "yes", do not complete rest of form.	6		
7	Were you the beneficiary of a plan participant who died? - If "no", see instructions on official Form 4972	7		
8	If the beneficiary of a participant who died after 1986, did you previously use Form 4972? - If "yes", do not use this form.	8		

Fig. 4.4 - The Check-box Questions on Form 4972 for Special Averaging

taxed as an annuity. Payments are made on a monthly basis for a term of years certain, or for life or lives. All annuity payments received are includible in gross income, except to the extent that a portion represents a return of premium or other consideration paid (such as your after-tax contributions to the plan). The payments are made under a contract which is bought by the plan after you signify your choice as to regular intervals of payment.

The term "annuity" is defined with reference to accepted standard usage within the insurance industry. This usage involves contracts such as life insurance, endowments, and annuities. The contracts provide for payments at regular (monthly) intervals over either a definite or an indefinite period of time. The indefiniteness is stated in terms of the life expectancy of the annuitant(s). The net effect is that a distributee has three annuity options to choose from. These options are—

1. Term of years certain
   — provides highest monthly payments (up to 10 years).
2. Single life
   — pays over the full life expectancy of the annuitant.
3. Joint and survivor
   — pays a specified amount for life of the first annuitant; when he dies, pays (usually a reduced amount) for life of the second annuitant.

What type of annuity payout is best for you? That depends on your immediate financial needs, your age and health, and whether you want to have some residual for your spouse. If you are married, the tax rules require that you accept a joint and survivor annuity unless your spouse consents otherwise.

If you choose a "years certain" annuity, you are guaranteed a certain total payout, called: *expected return.* If you die before the guaranteed period, your spouse, children, or other beneficiaries get the remainder in one lump sum. Any of these beneficiaries can take the lump sum and convert it into an annuity of his/her own.

If you choose an "indefinite" annuity — single or joint life — you are guaranteed a payout until end of life. If you or your joint annuitant dies before the age(s) indicated in actuarial tables, the insurance company administering the contract gets the remainder. If you live longer than the actuarial tables, you make money. The company still has to pay you or your surviving spouse indefinitely. The advantage of a life annuity is that you don't have to worry about outliving your money or squandering your retirement savings on bad investments.

Figuring Your "Expected Return"

For each plan which offers annuity-type distributions, the administrator is required to provide you with a statement of the monthly payments you can expect, for each annuity option covered. Other than indicating the cumulative amount of your after-tax contributions to the plan (if any), the administrator need provide no other information. He is not required to provide actuarial information as to what you can expect to receive, cumulatively, under each annuity type. You have to figure the expected return on your own, or get professional advice. Doing so for each annuity choice is the first step towards making your actual selection.

Figuring the expected return on an annuity requires the use of actuarial tables. Where do you get these tables?

Answer: From the IRS. Look in your phone directory for IRS Tax Forms. There's an 800 number there you can use. Call it and ask for **Publication 939**: Pension General Rule (Nonsimplified Method). Also ask for **Publication 575**: Pension and Annuity Income (Including Simplified General Rule). Publication 939 contains actuarial tables listing *Expected Return Multiples*, for each age and sex, single life and joint life. There are about 50 such tables, so read the headings carefully.

The tables in Publication 939 are arranged in two groupings: (A) plan contributions made before July 1986, and (B) plan contributions made after June 1986. On July 1, 1986 the IRS adopted unisex annuity tables. The unisex mortality rates are based on longer life expectancies of both men and women. For a given age, 65 for example, the comparative return multiples are:

Tables (A)	— male	15.0
	— female	18.2
Tables (B)	— unisex	20.0

The publications explain which tables you can use and why. Generally, Tables (A) apply when payments are made from a commercially purchased annuity independent of an employer-sponsored plan. Tables (B) apply to payments from a qualified employee plan, a qualified employee annuity, or a tax-sheltered annuity.

The tabulated expected return multiples are *years* of life expectancy. Consequently, when figuring the expected return on your annuity arrangement, the monthly payments must be multiplied by 12. This annual amount is then multiplied by the "multiplier" in the applicable table(s). Understand that expected multiples are just that: "expected," but not guaranteed. Enter the tables for the age nearest your annuity starting date.

For example, at age 65, suppose your first annuity payment is expected to be $1,800 per month. For a single life, the return multiple is 20.0 (unisex). Thus, your total expected return is:

$1,500 x 12/yr x 20 yrs = $360,000

For a joint life annuity, select the multiplier for the joint lives, then subtract from it the multiplier for the older life. The difference is the survivor's multiple. To illustrate, you are 65 and your spouse is 62. While you both are alive, you'll receive $1,200 per month; after you go, your spouse will receive $750 per month. From this information, your total expected return is determined as follows:

Your joint life multiple is 26.5 (ages 65–62)
Your single life multiple is <u>20.0</u> (age 65)
          difference is   6.5

Hence,

$1,200 x 12/yr x 20.0 yrs	=	$288,000
$ 750 x 12/yr x 6.5 yrs	=	<u>58,500</u>
Your total expected return	=	$346,500

Figuring Your "Exclusion Percentage"

Except in those cases where your employer contributed everything to your plan, you are not taxed on 100% of your annual payments. This is because adjustments are made for certain exclusions from tax. The three most common adjustments are:

- Your after-tax contributions to the plan.
- Death benefit exclusion, if included in the plan.
- Guaranteed refund feature, if included in the plan.

The adjustment amounts are returned to you, tax free. However, they do NOT come off the top. They are returned to you ratably (proportionately) over the duration of your annuity contract. The tax-free portion is expressed as an *exclusion percentage* of each annuity payment you receive. Once computed, your exclusion percentage remains fixed for the entire annuity duration.

In statutory language, your exclusion percentage is identified as a **ratio**. As such, it becomes a multiplying factor which applies to every payment you receive. The ratio factor is used to separate the nontaxable part from the taxable portion of your annuity.

The taxation of annuities is prescribed by Section 72 of the Internal Revenue Code. This 9,000-word tax law consists of 23 subsections (a) through (w). The general rule is subsection 72(a) which reads:

Except as otherwise provided . . ., gross income includes any amount received as an annuity (whether for a period certain or during one or more lives) under an annuity, endowment, or life insurance contract.

The phrase "except as otherwise provided" is intended to except the exclusion ratio. This ratio is defined in subsection 72(b)(1) as—

*Gross income **does not include** that part of any amount received as an annuity . . . which bears the same **ratio** to such amount as the investment in the contract (as of the annuity starting date) bears to the expected return under the contract (as of such date). [Emphasis added.]*

This definition boils down to the ratio (or percentage) of your after-tax investment in the contract to your total expected return.

Your investment in the contract constitutes your after-tax contributions to the plan, minus a guaranteed refund feature, if any. The guaranteed refund feature applies only to term certain annuities. Otherwise, for your own taxation purposes, your investment in the contract is the cumulative total of all your after-tax contributions to your employer-sponsored plan. The plan administrator is supposed to keep track of these contributions, and notify you each year of the totals to date. You should verify the information on your own.

To illustrate, suppose the plan administrator provided you with a statement that your cumulative after-tax contributions amounted to $85,000. The plan calls for your being paid $1,500 per month for life at age 65. Your expected return, as computed previously, is $360,000 . . . assuming that you do not die prematurely. Your exclusion ratio or percentage becomes—

85,000 ÷ 360,000 = 0.2361 or 23.61%

Hence, of each $1,500 payment received, $354 is tax free. The $1,146 balance ($1,500 – 354) is fully taxable.

In Figure 4.5 we summarize the annuity options and tax treatment of ordinary distributions from a qualified retirement plan. Typically, these are periodic "required distributions" when a plan participant reaches his/her normal retirement age.

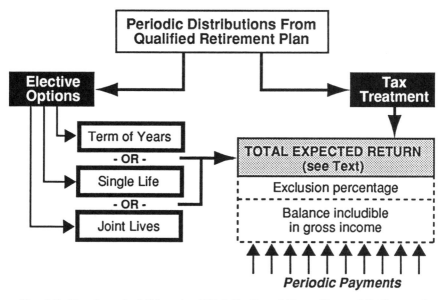

Fig. 4.5 - Treatment of "Required Distributions" Upon Normal Retirement

Tax-Sheltered Annuities

The above discussion on plan distribution options focuses on Section 402: Taxability of Beneficiary of Employee's Trust. Similarly, Section 403: Taxation of Employee Annuities, deals with distributions from tax-sheltered annuities (TSAs). A TSA — also known as a 403(b) plan — is a special type of retirement and deferred compensation plan. It is special in the sense that it applies only to employees of public schools, churches, scientific foundations, charitable organizations, and hospital cooperatives. The arrangement provides for investing funds in annuity contracts, mutual funds, and retirement income accounts. A TSA also permits more liberal contributions by employers and employees than do 402-type plans.

Distributionwise, there is a key difference between a 402 and a 403 TSA plan. A TSA cannot be rolled over into a 402 plan; it can only be rolled over to another TSA or to an IRA. A TSA plan cannot qualify for lump-sum special averaging treatment even if a lump-sum distribution is made. For annuity treatment, "investment in the contract" — the exclusion percentage — is computed similarly to a 402 plan (but with more factors considered). Basically, a TSA plan is set up to be an annuity plan throughout.

As each TSA employee becomes eligible, the employer immediately purchases an annuity contract with an insurance company. When distributions are made, Section 403(a)(1) states very clearly that—

. . . the amount actually distributed to any distributee under the contract shall be taxable to the distributee (in the year in which so distributed) under section 72 (relating to annuities).

The taxable portion of a TSA distribution is figured the same way as any other annuity distribution (discussed above). There are just more factors to consider when computing the nontaxable exclusion part. There are five such factors, namely:

(1) any excess employer contributions which were taxable to the participant during the cumulative plan years;
(2) any amounts taxable to the participant due to change of rights from forfeitable to nonforfeitable;
(3) any amounts contributed by the participant out of his own funds;
(4) any premiums paid by the employer to furnish the participant with life insurance protection; and

(5)   any loans to the participant by the plan that were included in participant's gross income.

Obviously, a lot more recordkeeping is required for a TSA plan by the administrator than for a 402-type plan. Otherwise, a TSA distributee has the same recipient options as any other annuitant. He can take his distributions for a term of years certain, for ordinary single life, or for joint and survivor lives. The actuarial tables for determining one's "expected return" are the same, whether Section 402 or Section 403 distributions are involved.

401(k) Plan Distributions

401(k) plans are referred to as *elective deferral agreements* or CODAs (Cash or Deferred Arrangements). They are "elective" in the sense that an employee chooses to make contributions on his own. He is under no obligation to do so, and may change his mind upon due notice to his employer. He makes the election by agreeing to take a reduction in compensation (salary, wages, commissions) to the extent of the qualifying contributions made. The amount of one's elective before-tax contributions is limited to approximately $9,000 per year. We say "approximately" because the actual limit is based on a complex aggregation formula involving all employee participants and inflation adjustments.

In general, unless a 401(k) distribution is rolled over to an IRA or used to purchase an annuity contract, all distributions are taxed by inclusion in gross income in the year of actual receipt. Ordinarily, they are not eligible for lump-sum averaging unless integrated with pension, profit-sharing, and stock bonus plans.

By far, most 401(k) distributions are for purposes *other than* normal retirement. This is because the distributions are not conditioned upon attaining a certain age or completion of a stated number of years of service. This is also because the contributory accumulations are employees' money (deferred compensation) held in custodial accounts administered by the employer rather than by an independent trustee.

Other than retirement, death, disability, or other separation from service, distributions may be made upon—

(1)   inadvertent excess contributions to the plan;
(2)   termination of the plan by the employer;
(3)   sale of substantially all assets of the business;
(4)   bankruptcy or liquidation of the business; or
(5)   immediate hardship needs of a participant.

Hardship distributions require compliance with Regulation 1.401(k)-(1)(d)(2): Employee's Hardship. The essence of this regulation is that the distribution is necessary to satisfy an immediate and heavy financial need of the employee. Qualifying needs are medical expenses, down payment on the purchase of a residence, up to 12 months' tuition, expenditures to stave off eviction or foreclosure, and amounts necessary to pay taxes and penalties on the distribution. The regulation instructs the employer to accept the employee's representation that the need cannot be met by insurance, liquidation of assets, or cessation of elective contributions.

Alternate Payees and QDROs

Section 401(a)(13): Assignment and Alienation, prohibits a retirement plan from being assigned or transferred to alternate payees, and from being subject to attachment, garnishment, or levy. However, there are two key exceptions to this anti-alienation provision. One exception (of course!) is any federal tax levy or unpaid assessment by the IRS. The other major exception is a Qualified Domestic Relations Order (QDRO). A QDRO requires a transfer of retirement benefits incident to marital divorce.

As defined in Section 414(p), a QDRO is a judgment, decree, or order made pursuant to a state's domestic relations or community property laws. The order is "qualified" if it clearly designates the following items:

(1)   name and address of each alternate payee, such as the spouse, former spouse, a child, or other dependent of the plan participant;
(2)   the amount or percentage of the participant's benefits to be paid to each alternate payee;

(3) the number of payments or the period to which the order applies; and

(4) each plan to which the order applies.

QDRO distributions from a plan are treated as annuity-type payments, and taxable as such to each recipient. However, if an alternate payee is a spouse or former spouse, the rollover option applies. This is NOT the case for children or other dependents who are alternate payees under a QDRO.

As with any annuity or rollover treatment, the after-tax component of a QDRO distribution has to be separated out. The targets of separation are the after-tax contributions and other tax includibles of the employee participant. The total after-tax component is apportioned on a pro rata basis between the QDRO value of the benefits and the total value of all benefits in the plan. The after-tax proration is applicable to the spousal payee only; nonspousal payees have to pay tax on their full distributions [Sec. 72(m)(10)]. The QDRO distributions do NOT affect the distribution options that the employee participant has with regard to the balance of his plan account.

Early Distribution Penalties

All plan distribution options have one tax trap in common. This trap is the 10% early distribution penalty prescribed by Section 72(t) of the IR Code. Section 72, recall, is the general taxation rule applicable to annuities of all types. Specifically, subsection 72(t)(1): Additional Tax on **Early Distributions**, reads—

*If any taxpayer receives any amount from a qualified retirement plan . . ., the taxpayer's tax . . . for the taxable year in which such amount is received **shall be increased** by an amount equal to 10 percent of the portion of such amount which is includible in gross income.* [Emphasis supplied.]

Tax deferred retirement plans are expressly for retirement purposes only. They are not a source of funds to be tapped for every financial need, imagined or real. As the employer-employee contributions grow and compound tax-free, there is always temptation to use the money as a bonus source whenever legitimate distributions occur. To dampen this temptation and to encourage rollovers, Section 72(t)(1) was enacted. The 10% is a flat add-on tax to all distributions that are not statutorily excepted.

Subsection 72(t)(2) prescribes the statutory exceptions as those distributions which are made—

(i)   *on or after the date on which the employee attains age 59¹/2,*

(ii)   *to a beneficiary (or to the estate of the employee) on or after the death of the employee,*

(iii)   *attributable to the employee's being disabled . . . [and] unable to engage in any substantial gainful activity,*

(iv)   *part of a series of substantially equal periodic payments . . . made for the life . . . or the joint lives . . . of the employee and his designated beneficiary,*

(v)   *to an employee after separation from service after attainment of age 55,*

(vi)   *dividends paid with respect to . . . employer securities which are held . . . by an employee stock ownership plan,*

(vii)   *to an alternate payee pursuant to a qualified domestic relations order.*

If you are involved in an early distribution and want to claim any of the exceptions above, you must prepare **Form 5329** and attach it to your regular Form 1040 for the year of distribution. Form 5329 is titled: Additional Taxes Attributable to Qualified Retirement Plans (Including IRAs), Annuities, and Modified Endowment Contracts. In general, the term "early distribution" refers to any distribution you receive before reaching age 59¹/2. This age definition is a reminder that the whole purpose of a tax-deferred retirement plan is to provide a source of income when reaching normal retirement age . . . and not before.

5

DISTRIBUTIONS FROM IRAs

> Some Confusion Exists Concerning Deductible, Nondeductible, And Spousal IRAs. Nevertheless, The Main Virtue Of An IRA Is As A RECEPTOR For Employer Plan Rollovers . . . Of All Types. Any Excess Contributions Have To Be Corrected. Between Ages $59^1/2$ And $70^1/2$, Distributions From IRAs May Be Of The NONANNUITY Type. They May Be Of Any Amount And Frequency Not Exceeding $150,000 Per Year. National Policy For Year 2000 Favors Greater Use Of IRAs For Retirement And Personal Savings. After $70^1/2$, Distributions Must Be Of The Annuity Type Until Your IRA Account Is Exhausted.

An IRA, including SEP/IRAs, is a self-directed *individual* retirement account. The exempt entity housing the contributed funds may be a trust or an annuity. Either way, once the contributions are made, the choice and allocation of assets for investment purposes are at the sole discretion of the account holder. An "account holder" is any individual, employed or self-employed, who earns compensation for performing personal services to others. The national trend favors greater uses of IRA accounts for supplementing the limitations of social security.

Unlike employer-sponsored plans that we covered in Chapter 4, IRAs are self-sponsored and self-directed plans. Even SEP/IRAs, employer association IRAs, and labor union IRAs are still considered self-sponsored. This is because, before any employer contributions can be made, the individual worker must set up his once the employer contributions are made, including rollover contributions from qualified employer plans, they are nonforfeitable. They are entirely under the self-direction of the account holder.

This self-direction aspect is what makes all distributions from IRAs a more confusing process than employer-sponsored plans. Unless the account holder is self-disciplined in financial matters and truly understands the role of IRAs in his retirement future, the tendency is to treat all IRA funds as a tax-free pool of money to do with what one wants. This is the danger of IRAs: the money can be dissipated before retirement.

Introduction to the IRA Concept

Congress first instituted the IRA concept in 1974. In that year, it enacted Public Law 93-406: *Employee Retirement Income Security Act*. That Act created Section 408 of the Internal Revenue Code: *Individual Retirement Accounts*. Section 408 was effective for taxable years beginning after December 31, 1974. Thus, the very first individual contributory year was 1975.

Section 408 recognized the fact that employers, large or small, when pressed by competition of the market place, would deny or diminish any retirement promise they made to their run-of-the-mill employees. The result was that many retiring employees were left with little or no retirement funds to supplement their social security benefits. The IRA concept became a means by which each worker could supervise and control his own retirement destiny. If started soon enough in one's employment life, IRAs constitute one of the most opportunistic and flexible retirement planning and income tools that an individual can have.

Section 408 comprises approximately 6,500 statutory words, arranged in 16 subsections: (a) through (p). The basic thrust of the IRA concept is embodied in subsection (a), to wit:

The term "individual retirement account" means a trust [or annuity] *created or organized in the United States for the exclusive benefit of an individual or his beneficiaries, but only if the written governing instrument creating the trust* [or annuity] *meets* [certain] *requirements.* [Emphasis added.]

The statutory requirements listed in Section 408(a) are that:

1. The trustee or custodian must be a bank, insurance company, or other financial institution (mutual fund, credit union, brokerage house) with a prototype IRA trust approved by the IRS.

2. The individual's interest in the account must be fully vested (nonforfeitable) at all times.

3. No part of the account may be used to buy life insurance.

4. If an annuity account, the contract must not be transferable by the owner.

5. The assets of the account may not be commingled with other property, except in a common trust fund or common investment fund.

6. The owner must begin to receive distributions from the account not later than age 70$1/2$.

7. The trustee or custodian cannot accept individual contributions of more than $2,000 during the year, and the contributions must be in cash.

8. In the case of contributions by an employer under a SEP arrangement, the trustee or custodian may accept greater amounts than $2,000 per taxable year, as permitted by the SEP rules (up to 15% of compensation or $30,000).

9. In the case of rollover contributions from a qualified employer plan, the contribution need not be in cash, and there is no limit on the amount of the rollover contribution.

An individual may have more than one IRA account at the same time. But if he does so, the annual contributory limits ($2,000 etc.) are applied as though there were one grand IRA in the aggregate.

Keep Spousal IRAs Separate

A general misconception prevails concerning spousal IRAs. Because married individuals may file an income tax return (Form 1040) jointly, there is belief that they can also establish a joint IRA account. This is NOT the case. Each IRA account must be kept separately, whether the account holders are married or not. An IRA account is a *per worker* plan.

For further clarification on this point, take out your latest Form 1040 (or 1040A). At the lower portion of its page 1, glance at the section headed: *Adjustments to Income*. There, you'll see two separate line entries. Each is labeled—

Your IRA deduction $_____
Spouse's IRA deduction $_____

This separation requirement is set forth in Section 219(f)(2). This section deals with IRA deductions for married individuals, and reads in key part—

> *The maximum deduction* [allowed: $2,000] *shall be computed separately for each individual, and . . . shall be applied without regard to any community property laws.*

If both spouses are working and each is earning $2,000 or more, and neither is covered by a qualified employer plan, then each separately may contribute $2,000 to his/her own account. Or, one spouse may contribute, and the other may not.

In the case of a nonworking spouse, Section 219(c) comes into play. This section is titled: Special Rule for Certain Married Individuals. The essence of this rule is that, if the working spouse earns at least $2,250 or more, and is not covered by a qualified employer plan, he may contribute $2,000 to the nonworking spouse's IRA, and $250 to his own. Or, vice versa. Or, $1,125 equally to each spousal IRA.

In the case of divorce, if a nonworking former spouse receives alimony, said alimony is treated as "compensation" under Section 219(f)(1). In such event, if the amount of alimony is $2,000 or more in a given year, up to $2,000 can be contributed to the divorced spouse's IRA.

One other note on spousal IRAs. There is NO PROVISION permitting the voluntary rollover of assets from one spousal IRA to the other spouse's IRA. Any such rollover is treated as a distribution includible in the transferring spouse's gross income. Tax and (possibly) penalties apply.

Contributory Confusion: Deductible IRAs

Congress — and the IRS — have really botched things up concerning the whole IRA process. When first enacted into law, it was a grand idea whose time was long overdue. But statutory changes and administrative spurs have crept into the concept to make it confusing for individual contributors. To this day, many of the rough edges as to what constitutes valid IRA deductions have not been smoothed out.

When IRAs started in 1975, the direct contributory amount per qualifying worker was $1,500 (per year). Said amount became an off-the-top deduction (called: "adjustment") to gross income, and any earnings thereafter were tax deferred until distributions were made. Virtually every worker took advantage of this concept. It was one of those rare Acts of Congress where the average taxpayer got some benefit out of the tax laws.

In 1981, the IRS complained to Congress that the Treasury Department was losing revenue because of the IRA rush. Commencing in 1982, Congress decided to prohibit direct IRA contributions where a worker **or** his spouse was covered by a qualified employer plan. For those not covered by such a plan, the direct contribution amount was increased to $2,000.

Following this 1982 change, there was an uproar over discontinuing a good idea at the urging of the IRS. As a result, commencing in 1987, Congress reinstated the IRA concept for all workers . . . but tacked on stringent new qualifying rules. Workers **and** their spouses who are NOT covered by a qualified employer plan are not affected by the 1987 rules.

The 1987 IRA rules imposed a means test on all workers **or** their spouses covered by an employer plan. The testing reference was — and still is — the AGI (Adjusted Gross Income) of the taxpayer as per his Form 1040 (or 1040A) filing status. The AGI is determined (for means testing purposes only) *without* regard to any allowable IRA deductions. The statutory AGI tests are:

A. Full IRA deduction — Single: $25,000 or less
Married: $40,000 or less
B. Partial IRA deduction — Single: less than $35,000
Married: less than $50,000
C. No IRA deduction — Single: $35,000 or more
Married: $50,000 or more

Needless to say, all of the above has added uncertainty and confusion concerning the validity of deductible IRAs. The IRS has prepared various worksheets to try to overcome the situation, but the worksheets have not been of much help. The confusion still remains as depicted in Figure 5.1. The result is that many taxpayers under about age 45 have given up or curtailed their direct IRA contributions, whether covered by an employer plan or not.

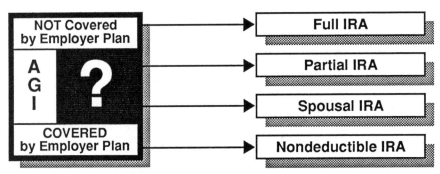

Fig. 5.1 - Confusion Aspects of Direct Contributions to IRAs

In early 1997, Congress recognized the growing disenchantment with IRAs. It began considering legislation to vastly improve the IRA concept by year 2000. The goal is to phase out all restrictions on deductible IRA contributions, and to allow full spousal IRA deductions for nonworking spouses. The intent, obviously, is to encourage greater use of deductible IRAs for retirement savings by individuals.

Nondeductible IRAs: New Concept

In 1987, the concept of a *nondeductible* IRA was introduced into our tax world. Whether covered by an employer plan or not, any individual worker could contribute up to $2,000 to an IRA account, nondeductibly. This is so prescribed by Section 408(o): *Rules Relating to Nondeductible Contributions to Individual Retirement Plans.*

A nondeductible IRA means that you get no current-year deduction for the contribution, but once in your IRA account, its earnings accumulate tax deferred. In other words, a nondeductible IRA is an after-tax contribution.

It is not clear who originated the nondeductible IRA concept: the IRS or Congress. For the IRS, nondeductibles make more tax paperwork and more tax regulations which the IRS loves. For Congress, the concept was a political sop to higher income workers who exceeded the deductible IRA thresholds. The statutory wording [Sec. 408(o)(2)(B)] limiting the amount which is nondeductible is very unclear. It uses the phrase *designated nondeductible contribution*, which is construed to mean $2,000 less any valid deductible amounts. If the nondeductibles were greater in amount than $2,000 per worker — say, in the $5,000 range — they'd make more sense as an inducement to really encouraging early savings for retirement.

If one does make a nondeductible IRA contribution for any taxable year, Section 408(o)(4) requires that the designated amount be shown on his tax return. For this showing, **Form 8606**: Nondeductible IRAs, is required to be attached to your return. The primary purpose of this form is to claim and track your cumulative **IRA basis** (after tax) for all of your contributory nondeductible years. Otherwise, if you fail to file the form and claim properly your IRA basis, you wind up paying tax a second time on the nondeductible amounts contributed. Form 8606 is a backhanded way (IRS's brainstorm) for disallowing full withdrawal of the nondeductible amounts without some tax or penalty.

In 1997, Congress entertained another version of the nondeductible IRA. This is the "IRA Plus" account. The details are yet to be worked out, but the idea seems to be to allow greater nondeductible contributions (up to $5,000 per year) with complete segregation of deductible and nondeductible IRA accounts. Complete segregation would eliminate Form 8606, and would exclude special purpose distributions from gross income. A "special purpose" distribution is for medical expenses, higher education expenses, long-term unemployment, and starting a new business by the IRA Plus owner.

Rollovers: The Real IRA Virtue

Most workers do not take IRA retirement savings seriously until they reach about age 45. This corresponds to about midway in their 40-year employment careers. By this time, they've worked with several or more employers and have acquired nonforfeitable (vested) rights to one or more employer plans. Upon separation from each job with a plan, every worker is faced with the decision of what to do with his vested assets. This is where the IRA concept really proves its worth. Instead of taking the money and property and paying tax (and penalties) on it, he can — and should — roll it over into his own individual IRA account. If he doesn't have an already existing account, he can contact his bank or other financial institution of his choice and set up one.

As an individual, you can have any number of separate IRA rollover accounts that you wish. There is no limitation on the number of said accounts. However, there is a limitation on what constitutes an "eligible rollover contribution." We discussed these limitations in the early portion of Chapter 4.

Rollovers from employer plans and from IRAs to IRAs are authorized by Section 408(d)(3): Rollover Contributions. Our depiction of the general rollover scheme that the IRA concept envisions is presented in Figure 5.2. The accommodation of rollovers is truly the masterpiece virtue of IRA. Rollovers can continue at any age up until 70$1/2$. After that age, there are mandatory distributions which we'll discuss later.

Generally speaking, a transfer of assets from an employer plan to an IRA is not treated as a distribution from the employer plan, nor is it treated as a contribution to an IRA plan. That is, if the transaction is accomplished within 60 days. It is simply a shifting

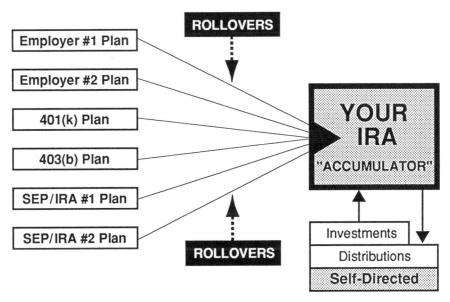

Fig. 5.2 - Rollovers: The Real Virtue of the IRA Concept

of custodianship from one trustee to another trustee. Because of withholding rules and the IRS's computer tracking of all financial affairs, direct trustee-to-trustee rollovers are much preferred.

Great care is required when instructing a trustee to make an eligible rollover transfer. Actually, there are two trustees to contact and instruct. There is a resigning trustee (existing plan custodian) and a receiving trustee (intended IRA custodian). Most trustees have their own preprinted IRA Transfer Authorization forms for executing a rollover. Get the receiving trustee's form and have it signed by the resigning trustee. Instruct the resigning trustee to computer log the transfer as **Code G**. The "Code G" is IRS computer language for: *Direct rollover to an IRA*. Insist that the resigning trustee do this properly. Otherwise, the IRS will pick up the transfer in its computer-matching fervor and tax you on the total amount transferred. Eligible rollovers are not taxable distributions. But you may have to prove this to the IRS if the transfer is not properly computer executed.

The reason that the IRS is fussy about rollovers is that IRAs are "self directed" accounts. This is all fine and good so long as prudent retirement goals are sought. But, when the self direction takes on the nature of self dealing, the account holder has crossed over into the domain tax classed as "prohibited transaction." This crossing over triggers certain sanctions called: *deemed distributions.*

Distributions of Excess Contributions

It is a fact that there *are* confusion and complications concerning the rules for deductible IRAs, nondeductible IRAs, SEP/IRAs, and eligible rollovers from employer plans. The situation often leads to what is tax classed as "excess contributions." Such excess is confusingly defined in Sections 4973(b)(1) and 408(d)(5) as any excess over $2,250 plus certain excess SEP amounts plus excess elective deferrals, plus ineligible components of employer-plan rollovers. Ineligible rollover contributions would be employee after-tax contributions, disqualified plan contributions, required annuity plan distributions, and nonspousal inherited accounts.

The problem with excess contributions is one of identity. Many IRA participants genuinely do not know what constitutes an excess contribution, or that an excess has been made. The only policing seems to be IRS computer-matching when an individual makes a direct contribution (deductible and nondeductible combined) in excess of $2,250 in a taxable year. Other excesses have to be discovered through information from employers, trustees, or tax professionals.

What happens if you've made excess contributions — knowingly or unknowingly?

The short answer is that you are subject to a 6% excise tax (penalty) for each year that the excess remains uneliminated. For computation of this penalty, you are expected to prepare and attach **Form 5329** (Part II). Form 5329 is titled: Additional Taxes Attributable to Retirement Plans (Including IRAs). Its Part II is titled: Tax on Excess Contributions to IRAs . . . a 9-step computational process.

The better answer is that you can avoid the penalty if you pursue the applicable corrective steps. There are three such steps, namely:

(1) Withdraw the excess amount *before* the due date of your return [Sec. 408(d)(4)].

(2)   Withdraw the excess amount after the due date of your return, by taking no deduction for the excess and reporting the earnings on the excess as ordinary income [Sec. 408(d)(5)(A)].

(3)   Withdraw the excess amount when it is discovered, file an amended return, and point out the excess was due to *erroneous information* conveyed at time of rollover [Sec. 408(d)(5)(B)].

When trying to correct excess contributions, you'll need the cooperation and understanding of your IRA trustee. You'll have to initiate the corrective action yourself by tracing and identifying accurately the excess amount. Request, instruct, and pray that the trustee will reverse his computer entries and, hopefully, advise the IRS of the corrective actions taken.

Treatment of Ordinary Distributions

An "ordinary" distribution from an IRA is one which is made after attaining age 59 1/2, and before attaining age 70 1/2. Distributions before age 59 1/2 are premature; those after 70 1/2 are delayed. Special penalties apply to early and to late distributions.

An ordinary distribution is also one which does not exceed $150,000 in a taxable year. We'll explain this later. In the meantime, to give a better perspective of the role of IRAs in your retirement future, we present Figure 5.3.

Except for the $150,000 annual distribution limitation, there is no minimum required amount that must be distributed between the ages of 59 1/2 and 70 1/2. This is a tremendous benefit which IRAs enjoy over employer plans. Under employer plans, when an employee reaches a plan-specified age (usually not less than 55 nor more than 70), the trustee must commence periodic payments (usually monthly) under the annuity rules. Such monthly distributions must be made whether the retiring employee wants them or not (except for rollovers and lump sums which we discussed in Chapter 4). The same requirement does not apply to IRAs until *after* age 70 1/2 is attained. Thus, an IRA participant

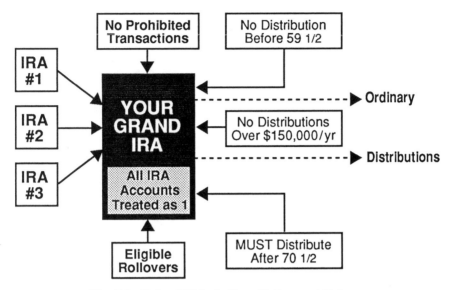

Fig. 5.3 - Role of IRAs in Your Retirement Future

(between 59 1/2 and 70 1/2) can withdraw or not withdraw from his IRA, depending on his actual needs from year to year. Because such withdrawals are not fixed and regular, they are treated as *nonannuity* distributions.

When an ordinary distribution (withdrawal) is made, it is includible in the IRA distributee's gross income under the Section 72 annuity rules. We discussed the annuity rules generally in Chapter 4. What we did not discuss in Chapter 4 was Section 72(e): *Amounts Not Received as Annuities*.

Nonannuity Distributions

If a distribution from an IRA is not considered to be an annuity payment, it is taxable under the rule of Section 72(e)(2). This general nonannuity rule reads (in part) that if an amount—

> . . . *is received before the annuity starting date*, [it]—
> *(i) shall be included in gross income to the extent allocable to income on the contract, and*

*(ii) shall **not** be included in gross income to the extent allocable to the **investment** in the contract.* [Emphasis added.]

In other words, under Section 72(e)(2), there is excluded from the recipient's gross income a *ratio amount* determined by the proportion of nondeductible contributions to the total value of the IRA at the close of the taxable year. The effect is that since one's cumulative nondeductible IRA contributions are after tax, they are not taxed again at time of distribution. This is that same exclusion percentage (or exclusion ratio) we illustrated in Chapter 4. Obviously, if, as an IRA participant, you made no nondeductible contributions whatsoever, you have no exclusion ratio to determine. In such case, the full distribution is included in gross income.

In applying the nonannuity rules, Section 408(d)(2) requires that—

(A) all IRAs be treated as one grand IRA,
(B) all distributions during the year be treated as one distribution, and
(C) the total value, income, and investment in the grand IRA be computed as of the close of the calendar year.

Consequently, if you haven't already done so, you should roll over all of your separate IRA accounts into one grand IRA before instituting your program of distributions.

When Distributing Nondeductibles

If you have made nondeductible contributions to your grand IRA account, you have some real homework to do. Your nondeductible contributions should come back to you as nontaxable distributions. To determine the nontaxable portion of each annual distribution, you have to plow through a moderately involved computational process. In the case of annuity-type distributions from an employer plan, this is done for you. But, in the case of an IRA plan, you have to do the computations yourself.

Let us illustrate what you have to do in simple terms. Suppose over 20 years of IRA participation you had contributed $5,000 in nondeductible IRAs, $10,000 in deductible IRAs, and $85,000 in rollover IRAs (from various employer plans). These contributions plus the tax deferred earnings thereon bring the total value of your grand IRA to $185,000. You are over $59^{1/2}$ when you withdraw exactly $5,000 from your grand account. Be aware that this distributed amount is exactly the same as your nondeductible contributions. Would this $5,000 come back to you completely nontaxable?

Surely you must know that the IRS never makes things this simple. So, the answer to the above question is: "No". The $5,000 distribution is partially — and minimally — nontaxable. In reality, it is *mostly* taxable. Here's why.

Based on the annuity rules exclusionary principle, the amount **nontaxable** would be:

$$\frac{5,000}{185,000} \times \$5,000 = 0.027 \times \$5,000 = \$135$$

The **taxable** amount would be:

$$\$5,000 - \$135 = \underline{\$4,865}$$

Obviously, the taxable amount is the lion's (and the IRS's) share.

Following this first distribution, your **IRA basis** (unrecovered nondeductible/nontaxable portion) is reduced to $4,865 ($5,000 initial – 135 recovered). Suppose you withdrew $5,000 the following year. How much would be nontaxable? Assume a 5% earnings rate on the $180,000 residual after the first $5,000 distribution. ($180,000 x 5% = $9,000; now, your total IRA value is $189,000.)

Of this second distribution, your nontaxable portion would be:

$$\frac{5,000}{189,000} \times \$5,000 = 0.0264 \times \$5,000 = \$132$$

And so on. At the same $5,000 annual distribution rate, it would take about 35 years to recover all of your nondeductible IRA contributions nontaxably. This is all procedurally sequenced for you on **Form 8606**: *Nondeductible IRAs (Contributions, Distributions, and Basis)*. Don't you see that this makes a lot more recordkeeping?

Premature Distributions

The problem with IRAs is one of perception with younger participants . . . those under 50. Most such persons regard IRAs not as part of their retirement intentions, but as short-term tax-sheltered savings. Since all IRAs are "self-directed," a participant can put his money in and take it out, at will. But he pays a price for this. He pays double. He pays his regular income tax on the distribution. Then he pays a 10% penalty on the distribution.

The 10% penalty for premature IRA distribution (under age 59 1/2) is prescribed by Section 72(t)(3)(A). The word penalty is softened somewhat by officially calling it an "additional tax." Its sole purpose is to discourage premature distributions and focus on the real purpose of IRAs, namely: retirement savings.

For IRAs, there are only three exceptions to the penalty. These exceptions are:

(1) Distributions caused by death of the participant.
(2) Distributions caused by disability of the participant in not being able to engage in any substantial gainful employment activity.
(3) Distributions that are part of a series of substantially equal payments over the participant's life expectancy or over the joint lives of himself and his beneficiary.

No other exceptions apply, no matter what the circumstances are. This "no other exceptions" rule was tested in Tax Court in the case of *A. J. Aronson*, 98 TC 283, Dec. 48,076. The case involved the distribution of all IRA proceeds from a failed savings and loan association. The Tax Court concluded that IRA funds paid out by an S&L receiver were includible in gross income and subject to the 10% penalty. Since the recipient was under 59 1/2, the court reasoned that he could have rolled the proceeds over within 60 days to another IRA, but he chose not to do so. This is tantamount to choosing to take the distribution prematurely.

The 10% penalty is computed by preparing **Form 5329**: Additional Taxes Attributable to . . . IRAs. Part I of the form, titled: *Tax on Early Distributions*, is used. Part I is a simple 4-step procedure which is quite self-explanatory.

Excess Distributions

The whole idea of tax deferred retirement savings is to provide a reasonable level of annual income during one's retirement years. Employer plans and IRAs were never intended to be a "loophole" for amassing huge sums of money tax deferred. Yet, it is not uncommon for highly compensated employees (corporate executives and others) to amass well over $1,000,000 to $3,000,000 in their retirement plans. When distributions are made from these plans, the annual amounts often exceed $150,000. In 1986, Congress posed the question: Does any retiree need more than $150,000 per year to live in reasonable comfort and security?

Congress decided that the answer was "No". It enacted an additional tax of 15% on all distributions exceeding $150,000 per year . . . after certain adjustments. This enactment became Section 4980A of the IR Code, effective for all distributions after August 1, 1986. This section is titled: *Tax on Excess Distributions from Qualified Retirement Plans*. This 15% penalty tax applies to IRA distributions as well as to those from employer plans. There are some exceptions for community property interests, investments in the contract, and distributions after death.

Section 4980A consists of six separate subsections comprising about 2,500 words. The substance is in subsections (a) and (b) which read essentially as—

There is hereby imposed a tax equal to 15 percent of the excess distributions with respect to any individual during any calendar year . . . reduced by the amount (if any) of the tax imposed by section 72(t) to the extent attributable to such excess distributions.

The reference to Section 72(t) is the 10% premature distribution penalty discussed above. The term "excess distributions" are those in excess of $150,000 [Sec. 4980A(c)(1)(A)].

The 15% penalty tax is computed by preparing **Part IV** of Form 5329: Tax on Excess Distributions from Qualified Retirement Plans (including IRAs). Part IV is a 9-step computational procedure requiring worksheets and frequent referencing to official instructions. The computation definitely requires professional assistance for those whose plan value exceeded $562,500 prior to August 1, 1986. For such retirees, a special grandfather rule applies which is beyond the scope of our discussion here.

Over 70^1/2: Distributions Required

In the same sense that retirement plans are not intended for amassing great wealth tax deferred, they are not intended as a means of saving money for one's heirs. In other words, retirement plans — IRAs and others — are NOT estate planning tools. The tax deferred accumulations are intended to be *consumption money.* This all goes back to the basic idea of taxing all plan distributions as an annuity. As an annuity, periodic payments are made until the distributee dies, or until his surviving spouse dies. At death, presumably, all plan benefits are exhausted.

Ordinarily, as an IRA account holder, you can make distributions or not make distributions as you see fit. BUT when you attain age 70^1/2, the rules change. You must make certain minimum required distributions . . . or face another penalty. This one is a whopper: 50%! It is prescribed by Section 4974(a) as an excise tax on *excess accumulations* in qualified retirement plans.

The 50% rate is intentionally made high to force you into consuming the money rather than saving it. At such a rate, what you may have intended for your heirs will be consumed by tax. This should make you think about when to start receiving your minimum required distributions.

Subsections 401(a)(9)(A) and (C) set the amount and date for the mandatory commencement of your IRA distributions. The date must commence no later than April 1 of the calendar year following the year in which you attain age 70$1/2$. This can be a confusing commencement date if your 70th birthday occurs after June 30.

If your 70th birthday occurs on or before June 30, you will be 70$1/2$ on or before December 31 of that year. Hence, you have three more months to April 1, to start receiving distributions.

On the other hand, if your 70th birthday occurs on September 30, 1997, say, you'll be 70$1/2$ on March 31, 1998. You than have until April 1, 1999 (the year following 70$1/2$) to commence mandatory minimum distributions.

Otherwise, you have to use **Part III** of Form 5329: Tax on Excess Accumulation in Qualified Retirement Plans (Including IRAs), to compute the 50% penalty. Part III is a simple 4-step procedure, namely:

Step 1 — Minimum required distribution $_____

Step 2 — Amount actually distributed   _____

Step 3 — Subtract Step 2 from Step 1   _____

Step 4 — Multiply Step 3 by 50% $_____

Attach Form 5329 to your regular Form 1040, and enter the Step 4 amount on its page 2 at the entry line marked: *Other Taxes; attach Form 5329*. Form 5329 has multiple "additional tax" uses as we have depicted in Figure 5.4.

Figuring Minimum Distributions

In the 4-step procedure above, you have to figure Step 1 (Minimum required distribution) before you can do Step 4. How do you determine your "minimum required distribution"? Hint: Keep in mind that, by April 1 of the year following your becoming 70$1/2$, your nearest age will be 71 or over.

Your minimum distributions are those required to exhaust the value of *all* of your IRA accounts upon your death, or upon your and your surviving spouse's deaths. If you have more than one IRA account, you'll have to compute the minimum for **each account**

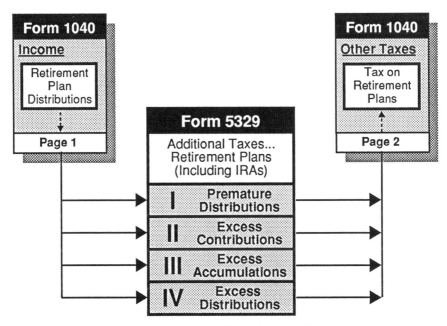

Fig. 5.4 - How Form 5329 "Attaches" to Form 1040

separately. This is why, earlier, we suggested combining all of your IRAs into one grand IRA. This way, you'll have to make only one distribution computation each year.

How will you know the value of your grand IRA at the end of each year? This is where **Form 5498**: IRA Information, comes in handy. The IRA trustee is supposed to provide you with a Form 5498 by January 31 following the close of each taxable year. In the center of the form there is a large box which reads—

Fair market value of account $_____.

This FMV is the amount that you have to exhaust over your actuarial life expectancy.

In Chapter 4, we told you of IRS-prepared actuarial tables that can be found in its **Publication 939**: Pension General Rule. You should have a copy of this publication for your own records. It gives "expectancy multiples" (in years) for single lives and joint lives. For annuity starting dates after June 30, 1986, unisex tables should be used.

Figuring your required minimum is a relatively simple procedure. To illustrate, suppose the FMV of your grand IRA is $250,000. For single life at age 71, your expectancy multiple is 15.3 years . . . or 184 months (12 mo/yr x 15.3 yrs = 183.6). Therefore, your minimum monthly distribution in your first post-70$1/2$ year must be—

$250,000 ÷ 184 months = $1,358 per month

If you have a spouse who is, say, three years younger than you, your first year's expected multiple would be 21.2 years or 254 months. Your minimum monthly distribution therefore becomes—

$250,000 ÷ 254 months = $984 per month

Each year, you have to refigure the monthly minimum. This is because each year you are one year older, and the value of your grand IRA has diminished by the prior year's consumption.

If looking up in the IRS's actuarial tables becomes too much for you, use the "safe harbor" (simplified) rule. Divide the FMV at the end of each preceding year by 120 months (10 years) and that becomes your minimum distribution. For the $250,000 value above, your required distribution would be—

$250,000 ÷ 120 months = $2,083 per month

The safe harbor rule permits you to divide the successively diminishing FMVs of your IRA account by the same 120 factor. You can use this divider year after year . . . until your IRA is exhausted.

6

UNDERSTANDING FORM 1099-R

When Any (Tax Deferred) Retirement Plan Money Or Property Is Distributed To You, The Payer Must Issue Form 1099-R. Box 1 Of This Form Displays The Gross Distribution; This Is The Only Amount The IRS Computer "Sees." Your Taxable Amount May Be — And Often Is — Less. Depending On Your After-Tax Contributions, Box 7 Is A MUST READ As It References 18 Different Informational Codes. Four Separate Spaces Appear On Form 1040/1040A For Entering The Form 1099-R Data. Care Is Always Required When Entering Any After-Tax Distributions — Especially IRAs And SEPs — On Your 1040s.

As a distributee from any kind of retirement plan, you'll receive a Form 1099-R from each plan . . . for each year that a distribution is made. If you receive distributions from several plans, you'll receive several 1099-Rs. Even if you receive independently an IRA or a SEP distribution, a Form 1099-R will be issued. This is analogous to receiving a Form W-2 from each employer for whom you worked during your occupationally active years. The distinguishing features are the letters "R" and "W". The "R" stands for Retirement Income; the "W" stands for Working Income. All income, as you know, has to be reported annually on Form 1040.

A key distinction between a 1099-R and a W-2 is where and how income is entered on your Form 1040/1040A. Your Form W-2 income is reported on the very first income entry line on your return. There is only one line and one space for such entry. In contrast, your Form 1099-R income is reported about 10 lines farther down. There are *two* lines for this reporting . . . and *four* spaces. It is because of these four entry spaces that we feel that a separate chapter is necessary to explain Form 1099-R to you.

Because of the physical similarity between Forms W-2 and 1099-R, there tends to be some confusion between the two. Each has a Box 1 which reports the gross amount paid to you. If you erroneously report the 1099-R gross amount in the W-2 line, as many often do in the first few years of retirement, you WILL overpay your tax. This is guaranteed! The IRS's computer will see to it that you overpay.

Thus, in this chapter, we want to focus on explaining why there are four entry spaces on your Form 1040 for the 1099-R amounts. We want to explain the differences between the four; we want to explain the tax traps involved; and we particularly want to explain the various *distribution codes* that you will find on Form 1099-R. Misreading or misinterpreting these IRS codes could result in your being computer terrorized at a time in your life when your attention should be on more enjoyable matters.

By our focusing in this chapter on Form 1099-R, we will also be conveying to you an important subliminal message. That message is: Entering the retirement phase of your life WILL NOT spare you from annual tax tracking by Big Brother. The reality is, you'll be tax tracked through 1099-Rs . . . until you die. Even then, your beneficiary may receive one or more 1099-Rs. The IRS just won't let you go in peace.

Introduction to Form 1099-R

You may have seen a Form 1099-R before. But we bet that you haven't studied it carefully. In some respects it is similar to a Form W-2; this often causes confusion. So, please take the time to read the full title of Form 1099-R. Its title alone conveys a lot about what the form covers. It reads:

Distributions from Pensions, Annuities, Retirement or Profit-Sharing Plans, IRAs, Insurance Contracts, Etc.

In short, the form reports distributions from pensions and annuities of all types, and distributions from IRAs including SEP/IRAs. The report is made first to you — the distributee/recipient — and then to the IRS. The form is prepared by the trustee, custodian, or administrator of each plan in which you are a participant at the time of any distribution.

The "Etc." in the Form 1099-R title covers some 28 other items which are not readily self-explanatory. Ten of the items are entered on the face of the form; 18 others are covered by computer code symbols. Much of this Etc. information is for your benefit in deciding how to compute and report (on Form 1040/1040A) the correct taxable amount of your gross distribution. The dollar amount in Box 1 of the 1099-R is the maximum amount taxable. Depending on specific provisions for participating in your plan, you may not have to pay tax on the Box 1 gross amount. This is where the Etc. data becomes important.

As a brief overview, Form 1099-R is divided into two halves, vertically. The left half contains all the payer and recipient information that you are accustomed to on tax forms: name, address, and Tax ID of payer; name, address, and Tax ID of recipient; and account or control number, as appropriate. It is the right-hand half of Form 1099-R that we specifically want to address. This is where all the information is that goes onto your tax return and into the IRS's Big Computer.

The right-hand half of Form 1099-R consists of 10 separate boxes of information. Not all of these boxes will be filled in your case; the fillings depend on the type of plan from which your distributions are made. In edited, abbreviated, and enlarged form, we present these 10 boxes to you in Figure 6.1. The official form doesn't look like our figure; yet, we have all the ingredients there.

Before we explain the most important boxes to you, we'd like for you to take a moment and actually read through the box headings in Figure 6.1. This short reading alone will provide useful information to you. But it may — and should — raise questions in your mind that you never thought about before. For example, Box 2b has two checkboxes within it, namely:

Taxable amount not determined ☐

1 Gross distribution $	Taxable Year _____	FORM 1099-R
2a Taxable amount $		

2b Taxable amount not determined ☐	Total distribution ☐
3 Capital gain (in box 2a) $	4 Federal tax withheld $
5 Employee contributions or insurance premiums $	6 Net unrealized appreciation in employer securities $

7 Distribution code	IRA/SEP ☐	8 Other $	%

9 Your percentage of total distribution _____ %

Fig. 6.1 - The 10 Boxes of Key Information on Form 1099-R

Total distribution   ☐

Do you have any idea what these checkboxes are getting at? We'll tell you in a moment.

The 4 Spaces on Form 1040

Before telling you what the two little checkboxes above are about, we must first call your attention to the retirement income lines on page 1 of Form 1040 (and 1040A). If you will look at page 1 of your latest federal return, you will see two separate line entries designated as—

- *Total IRA distributions $_____ ; Taxable amount $_____*
- *Total pensions and annuities $_____ ; Taxable amount $_____*

These are the four spaces that we alerted you to above.

Two messages should immediately pop out from these four spaces. One is that your IRA distributions are set apart from any distributions from pension and annuity (P&A) plans. The second message is that in either case, IRA or P&A, there is a taxable amount which may differ from that of the total (or gross) amount. How do you know if there is any difference?

In some cases, the plan administrator may compute the taxable amount for you. If he does so, he shows an entry in Box 2a of Form 1099-R (in Figure 6.1). If Box 2a is less than Box 1 (Gross distribution), the difference is nontaxable. We hasten to point out that Box 2a is only done for pensions and annuities. And it is not done in every case. In such event, there is no entry in Box 2a.

Box 2a is never done for IRAs or SEP/IRAs. For these distributions, you have to compute the taxable amount yourself. How do you do this?

Answer: You read the Instructions for Recipient — IRAs, on Form 1099-R. These instructions say, in part—

*For distributions from an IRA or SEP, the payer is not required to compute the taxable amount. Therefore, the amounts in Boxes 1 and 2a may be the same. See **Pub. 590**, Individual Retirement Arrangements (IRAs), and **Form 8606**, Nondeductible IRAs, to determine the taxable amount.*

This official instruction puts you out on a limb. If you can't figure the taxable amount properly, you have to report the gross distribution as the taxable amount. The IRS's computer only sees the gross amount as the taxable amount. If this is incorrect, you have to prove that the IRS is wrong. Now do you see why we said earlier that you can be easily overtaxed on your retirement distributions?

The Issuers of Form 1099-R

The trustee, custodian, or administrator of your retirement plan, whether employer-sponsored or self-sponsored, is the person required by law to prepare and issue Form 1099-R. The specific requirement is **Section 6047**: *Information Relating to Certain Trusts and Annuity Plans*. The highlights of this section can be surmised from its five principal subsections, namely:

(a)   Trustees and Insurance Companies
(b)   Owner-Employees
(c)   Other Programs [IRAs]
(d)   Reports by Employers, Plan Administrators, Etc.
(e)   Employee Stock Ownership Plans

The overall gist that we want you to be aware of is that these "custodians"—

... shall file such returns (in such form and at such times), keep such records, make such identification of contracts and funds (and accounts within such funds), and supply such information, as the [IRS] shall by forms or regulations prescribe. [Emphasis added.]

The phrase "by forms and regulations" refers to Form 1099-R, its instructions, and Regulation 1.6047-1. The essence of this single regulation is that—

A separate Form 1099-R shall be filed with respect to each payee. . . . The amounts subject to reporting . . . include all amounts distributed or made available . . . whether or not such amounts are includible in gross income. [Emphasis added.]

This emphasized phrase tells you three things "between the lines." One is that Form 1099-R is an *information* report only; it is not a tax computational return. Secondly, the issuer's responsibility is limited to reporting every amount that was actually paid or made available to you. And, thirdly, beyond reporting the aggregate or gross distribution, the issuer has no responsibility for how you use — or misuse — the information provided. So, don't blame the issuer for not doing your tax work for you.

No person really likes to read or study tax information forms prescribed by the IRS. Yet, Form 1099-R is a case where, if you do not do so, there are adverse consequences. Being aware of this, we'll try to narrow down our dissertation on the 10 boxes in Figure 6.1 to those items which are most important to you.

Boxes 1, 2a and 2b on 1099-R

We know that many of the following paragraphs will be humdrum and mundane. Nevertheless, we'll state right off that if you master Boxes 1, 2a, and 2b (and later Box 7) on Form 1099-R, you will have made much progress at beating the IRS at its own game. But if your eyes are glazing over at this stage, you have no choice but to pay tax on the gross amount shown in Box 1. If you are satisfied with doing this, you can skip the rest of this chapter.

If you do skip the rest of this chapter, believing that you made an eligible nontaxable rollover, how can you be sure that the IRS's computer will treat it as nontaxable? Either way, the Big Computer still only sees Box 1. Your only protection against the computer is understanding what the 1099-R boxes are all about. For a direct rollover, "zero" should be shown in Box 2a and code letters "G" or "H" should be shown in Box 7. For an **indirect** rollover, the 1099-R instructions tell you: *See Form 1040 or 1040A instructions: Rollovers — IRA and Rollovers — P&A.*

The instructions to Box 1 tell you that the amount shown—

> . . . *may have been a direct rollover or received as periodic payments, as nonperiodic payments, or as a total distribution. Report this amount on Form 1040 or 1040A . . . unless this is a lump-sum distribution and you are using* **Form 4972**, *Tax on Lump-Sum Distribution. . . .* [Form 4972] *does not apply to IRAs or tax-sheltered annuities. . . . If an insurance contract has been transferred to another trustee or contract issuer, an amount will be shown in this box* [Box 1] *and Code 6 will be shown in Box 7. You need not report this on your tax return.*

The instructions to Box 1 also tell you to report disability payments (if under minimum retirement age) and corrective distributions of excess contributions or excess deferrals (of compensation) on the line on Form 1040/1040A for "Wages, salaries, tips, etc." If you receive any employer-paid death benefits as a beneficiary of a deceased employee, you report this amount on Form 1040 on the line for "Other income."

The instructions to Box 2a: Taxable amount, tell you that—

If there is no entry in this box, the payer may not have all the facts needed to figure the taxable amount. In that case, the first box in Box 2b [Taxable amount not determined] *should be checked. . . . If the second checkbox* [in Box 2b] *is marked, the distribution was a total distribution that closed out your account.*

Otherwise, if Box 2a is blank and Box 2b also blank — as so often happens — you are left to your own devices on how to report the amount shown in Box 1. This is where Box 7 comes in. It is the real information provider of what is taking place in Box 1.

Box 7: Must Read

Generally, an entry in Box 1 tells you that a distribution has been made. The specific dollar amount is indicated. This is all that Box 1 tells you. This is all the IRS computer needs to max tax you. If you want to know more about the details of Box 1, you have to refer to Box 7.

Of the various boxes and entries on Form 1099-R, Box 7 is the most important one of all. It provides a lot of information that you cannot find elsewhere. It is a MUST READ box . . . even if you read no others.

As you can see in Figure 6.1, Box 7 has two subboxes within it. The second subbox contains the checkbox: ☐ *IRA/SEP*. If this checkbox is marked (usually with a small "x"), you know immediately that the distribution is from an IRA or SEP plan. This little marking puts you on official notice that you have to compute the taxable/nontaxable parts of the distribution strictly on your own. There are no other instructions accompanying the IRA/SEP checkbox.

The first subbox in Box 7 is labeled: *Distribution code*. All that will show here is a single alphanumeric symbol. There are 18 different code symbols that can be used: 9 numeric, 9 alphabetic Where do you find the meaning of these symbols?

Copy C of Form 1099-R is designated as: *For Recipient's Records*. On the reverse side of this copy, there are preprinted "Instructions for Recipient." These instructions are in very small —

and often very faint — print. Way down in the subfine print, there is a listing of code symbols for Box 7. The leadoff sentence reads—

These codes identify the distribution you received.

As stated above, there are 18 of these code symbols. Because they are squinched together so, we feel that you should see them in more readable, normal print size. Accordingly, Figure 6.2 is presented. Even a casual glance at Figure 6.2 should impress you with the diversity of information contained in Box 7. You just hope and pray that the symbols entered are correct. Not all issuers of Form 1099-R make the correct entries.

Box 7	Distribution Code	Form 1099-R
CODE	ITEM	
1	Early distribution, no known exception	
2	Early distribution, exception applies	
3	Disability of participant	
4	Death of participant	
5	Prohibited transaction	
6	Tax-free exchange of insurance contracts	
7	Normal distribution	
8	Excess contributions, current year	
9	Premiums paid for insurance, taxable	
A	Eligible for lump-sum averaging	
B	Exclusion of life insurance proceeds	
C	Eligible for both A and B	
D	Excess contributions, 2nd prior year	
E	Excess annual additions, taxable	
F	Charitable gift annuity	
G	Direct rollover to IRA	
H	Direct rollover to P & A plan	
P	Excess contributions, 1st prior year	

Fig. 6.2 - The 18 Code Symbols for Box 7 (1099-R)

If there is no entry in Box 7, you are in trouble. The issuer/payer has left you hanging out to dry. You are at the sole mercy of the IRS's computer. It will self-program all the penalties against you that it can. Your only recourse is to contact the payer to correct things.

Correcting Form 1099-R

As you can see in Figure 6.2, there are a lot of opportunities for the payer to make mistakes on your Form 1099-R. From your own knowledge of your plan and your participation therein, you should be able to tell fairly quickly if mistakes have been made. If there is a screwup, do not be alarmed. Errors happen all the time. Retirement plan rules are so complicated that it is a marvel that more errors are not made. You cannot spot them, of course, until after you have received your copy of the form.

You are supposed to receive a copy of Form 1099-R by January 31 following the close of each calendar year. Rarely are these forms issued on time. This can be frustrating if you have distributions from more than one plan. All IRA distributions have to be grouped together on one Form 1040 line; all P&A distributions have to be grouped together on a separate Form 1040 line. Your taxable year is the calendar year in which the distributions were actually received by you. Sometimes a payer will make a distribution in one year, and report it to the IRS in the following year. This can cause endless computer-matching problems between you and the IRS, and between you and the payer.

The most common errors are found in Boxes 1, 4, and 7. In Box 1, the payer may have reported a gross amount different from that which you actually received. Box 4 (Federal income tax withheld) is often left blank even though you may have instructed the payer to withhold. Or, if there is an entry in Box 4, it is far below what the actual tax on the distribution turns out to be. Box 7 (Distribution code) is where most of the payer errors are made. For your own protection, you must cross-check the code symbol reported with its identification in the official instructions. If the cross-check doesn't make sense, contact the payer.

If Form 1099-R is not received by January 31, or if, when received, there is an error, you must contact the payer. Hopefully you know — or can find out — who the payer is, or who his representative is. Make contact by phone and explain the situation the best you can. Follow up with a confirming written statement, keeping a copy for yourself and making a copy for the IRS. Don't expect the IRS to make any corrections on Form 1099-R for you. Only the payer can do this.

For the above purposes, Form 1099-R has a correction box at the very top of the form. This is a single checkbox which appears as follows:

☐ *CORRECTED (if checked)*

If you find any kind of error on your copy of Form 1099-R, insist that the payer re-issue the 1099-R with the correction box checked. Chances are, though, this will not take place until after you have filed your tax return. This is where a copy of your written statement to the payer to correct things can be attached. At least it will buy you some time with the IRS. Eventually, you will have to file an amended return, with a copy of the corrected 1099-R attached.

Other Boxes on Form 1099-R

We have covered above what we think are the most important boxes on a 1099-R. There are other boxes that we should at least touch on. Box 3, for example, *Capital gain*, only applies if you were born before 1936 and received a lump-sum distribution for which you qualify to use Form 4972: Special Averaging.

Box 4, *Federal income tax withheld*, is self-explanatory. However, Copy B of Form 1099-R (which is attached to your Copy C) carries the following bold-print instruction on its face:

Report this income on your Federal tax return. If this form shows Federal income tax withheld in Box 4, attach this copy to your return.

Unless there are tax withholdings, you do not normally have to attach the 1099-Rs to your 1040/1040A return. The IRS already has the information it wants, namely: the gross amount in Box 1.

Box 5, *Employee contributions or insurance premiums*, shows your after-tax contributions to the plan which are recovered tax free in the distribution year. Presumably, if the 1099-R was prepared properly, Box 1 less Box 2a should equal Box 5. You might cross-check this on your own. The instructions, however, say that—

This box does not show any contributions to an IRA or SEP.

Box 6, *Net unrealized appreciation in employer's securities*, is a mouthful. The acronym "NUA" is used for short. This is the increase in value of such securities while in the retirement plan trust. The NUA amount in Box 6 is NOT included in Box 1. You pay no tax on the NUA until you sell the securities which have been distributed to you.

Box 8, *Other*, applies to any annuity contracts received as part of the distribution. The value of the contract is shown, but it is NOT included in Box 1. The contract is not taxable until you start receiving periodic payments under its terms. If the distribution is made to more than one person, the percentage of the contract distributed to you is shown.

Box 9, *Your percentage of total distribution*, applies to those situations where there is more than one recipient of the plan benefits. Examples would be pursuant to a divorce decree, or upon death of a participant. At time of death of an employee, each beneficiary shares in the life insurance proceeds of that employee to the extent of the percentage in Box 9.

Box 7 Revisited

Previously, we indicated the computer importance of Box 7 and listed its 18 distribution variants in Figure 6.2. Our listing of the 18 separate codes is only a slight improvement over the official arrangement on Form 1099-R. In most cases, two codes are squeezed together on the same official line, making it difficult to decipher any thought or organization to the arrangement. Perhaps we can add a little rationale to the official arrangement.

Codes 1, 2, 3, and 4 deal with early (premature) distributions for participants under age 59^1/2. Code "1" stresses *no known exception; see Form 5329.* Form 5329 recall (in Chapter 5) is: Additional Taxes Attributable to Retirement Plans (etc.). It's that 10% penalty that the IRS computer is looking for. Code "2" indicates that an exception applies other than disability and death. Codes "3" and "4" signify disability and death, respectively. Codes 2, 3, and 4 are accompanied by the annotation: *You need not file Form 5329.*

There are two codes that signify eligible rollovers. However, both apply only to direct rollovers: trustee-to-trustee. Code "G" is a direct rollover to an IRA, whereas Code "H" is a direct rollover to a P&A plan. There are no code symbols signifying an indirect rollover. In such case, the only way to signify to the IRS that a qualified rollover has been made is to enter "zero" in the taxable amount space on page 1 of Form 1040/1040A. And, immediately above the words *taxable amount*, hand enter the word "Rollover." In order for the computer to recognize your rollover entry, you must also enter the Box 1 amount in the *Total distribution* space on Form 1040/1040A.

The Box 7 codes that signify penalties are: "**5**", prohibited transaction; "**8**", excess contribution current year; "**D**", excess contributions second prior year; and "**E**", excess annual additions. You want to be alert to these codes as this is where payer errors can cause you much computer pain.

The only entry in Box 7 that signifies normal distribution (over age 59^1/2) is **Code 7**. Don't get confused with Box 7 and Code 7. Ideally, for ordinary retirement purposes, the digit "7" is what you want to see displayed. This is your least computer troublesome code of all.

If your normal distribution from a P&A plan qualifies for special lump-sum averaging, Codes "A", "B", or "C" appear. Code "A" applies to 5- or 10-year averaging; Code "B" for certain death benefits; and Code "C" includes both "A" and "B". With "A" or "C" entered in Box 7, the IRS computer will be on notice to look for your Form 4972: Tax on Lump-Sum Distributions.

Items also treated as normal distributions are: Code "9", insurance premiums paid by the trustee, and Code "E", excess annual additions. Both items are taxable to you currently as P&A income.

There are two items for information purposes which have no immediate tax consequences. These are Code "6", tax-free exchange of insurance contracts, and Code "F", charitable gift annuity. You pay tax when you start receiving payments from these two items.

IRA Distributees: Get Pub. 590

As you can sense from our brief comments above, most of the Box 7 items pertain to distributions from employer-sponsored pension and annuity plans. For these plans, the trustee/custodian has most — if not all — of the information he needs to prepare and complete Form 1099-R properly. The trustees are paid by the employer to do the custodial and administrative tasks. Besides, larger employers have their own professional staffs who provide the trustees with the proper contributory data (before-tax and after-tax) and participant vesting information. Thus, the 1099-Rs issued by employer-sponsored plans are, on the whole, quite accurate. Most of the foulups occur in multiple trustee-to-trustee rollovers.

In the case of IRA accounts, very little administrative supervision is provided. Since IRAs are self-directed, each IRA distributee is pretty much on his own. This means that each IRA account holder has a lot more recordkeeping to maintain, and a lot more chances for trustee errors on his Form 1099-R. As an IRA holder, your recordkeeping tasks are particularly onerous if you have made nondeductible IRA contributions over a period of 5, 10, or more years.

In most IRA cases, the taxable amount in Box 2a of Form 1099-R is left blank. Box 2b (tax amount not determined) is often checked — but not always. Box 7, if not left blank, often shows Code "1" if under age 59$\frac{1}{2}$ or Code "7" if over age 59$\frac{1}{2}$, whether or not these code entries are correct. An IRA trustee simply has no way of knowing all the relevant facts concerning your IRA plan. Accordingly, an IRA trustee completes Form 1099-R the best he can, in order to get it out of his hands. He is under pressure from the IRS to get the forms out on time. If he fails to provide you with a 1099-R, he is subject to a $50 penalty *plus* $25 a day after January 31 [Secs. 6047(d), 6652(e), and 6704(b)].

When queried about the information on your 1099-R, an IRA trustee will respond by saying (or writing): "See your tax or financial advisor."

Before you do this, we strongly urge that you procure IRS **Publication 590**: *Individual Retirement Arrangements (IRAs)*. It is a 62-page document that deals strictly with IRAs and SEPs. It is one of the better informational publications that the IRS has ever produced. It is straight-headed and straightforward . . . with very little bureaucratese.

Publication 590 is full of all kinds of IRA information, starting with setting up and making contributions, to the tax treatment of your distributions. It has a particularly good section on figuring your taxable and nontaxable amounts of each year's gross distribution reported on Form 1099-R. It also has abbreviated actuarial (life expectancy) tables for figuring your minimum required distributions after attaining age $70^1/2$.

IRA Basis & Form 8606

There is one major shortcoming of Form 1099-R. It provides no **IRA basis** information whatsoever. This is where your own records are essential.

Your IRA basis is the total of all your *nondeductible* IRA contributions over the years, minus the total of all nontaxable IRA distributions received. It is a running tabulation of your after-tax contributions minus your nontaxable distributions, year after year, until your IRA account is depleted. The key document required for this purpose is **Form 8606**: *Nondeductible IRAs (Contributions, Distributions, and Basis)*. We introduced this form to you briefly in Chapter 5. Publication 590 gives you filled-in examples of using this form.

To help you visualize better the IRA basis concept, we present Figure 6.3. It is the main thrust of Form 8606 which supplements the information on Form 1099-R. We functionalize this concept so

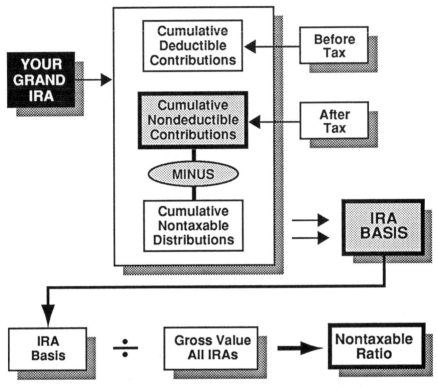

Fig. 6.3 - The IRA Basis Concept . . . and How Used

that you can see the mechanics of Form 8606 without getting bogged down in the frequent (5 times) "See instructions" directives on the official form.

Essential to completing Form 8606 in a year of distribution is the total value of your grand IRA account at the end of your distribution year. For each separate IRA account you may have, the trustee is required to provide you with **Form 5498**: *IRA Information* for that year. You total your various IRA values into one grand value, then ADD to that amount the distributions you received during the year. This gives you a denominator for establishing the nontaxable (exclusion) ratio applicable to your distributions. Your IRA basis divided by the total IRA value results in your exclusion ratio.

The rest of Form 8606 is straightforward. You multiply your distribution for the year by your exclusion ratio to get your nontaxable portion. The remainder of the distribution is taxable. This is the portion that you enter in the space for *Taxable amount* on page 1 of Form 1040/1040A.

From your IRA basis for the distribution year, you subtract the nontaxable distribution portion to arrive at a new IRA basis at the start of the following year. You have to continue with Form 8606 year after year until your entire IRA basis is recovered. Obviously, to prepare each Form 8606 properly, there is substantial ongoing recordkeeping required on your part. Form 8606 is a required attachment to your tax return; you need to do it right.

In Figure 6.4, we summarize the various "pieces" that go into establishing the *Taxable amount* of your IRA distributions. The only information you get from Form 1099-R is the gross distribution amount and a marked checkbox ☐ IRA/SEP. From this point on, you need the forms and data indicated in Figure 6.4.

State Taxables May Differ

All of the above pertains to the federal reporting and taxation of your retirement plan distributions. Omitted has been any discussion of state and local taxation matters. All states — and, in a few cases, some local agencies — want their bite out of your retirement income. We all tend to forget this when focusing on the IRS forms.

To accommodate state and local income tax agencies, Form 1099-R has six box spaces at its very bottom. They are designated as Boxes 10 through 15. Two boxes (10 and 13) are for tax withholdings; two boxes (11 and 14) are for state and local identifications); and two boxes (12 and 15) are for state and local distribution amounts.

The instructions to these six boxes are as follows:

If state or local income tax was withheld from the distribution, these boxes may be completed. Boxes 12 and 15 may show the part of the distribution subject to applicable state and/or local tax.

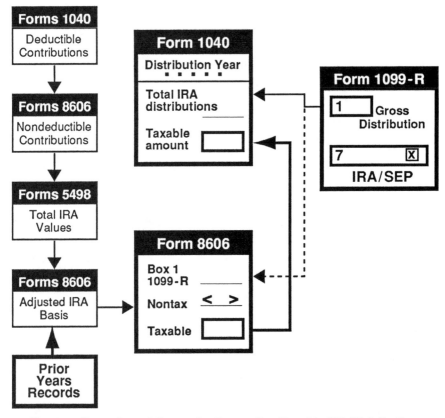

Fig. 6.4 - Records and Forms for Computing Taxable IRA Distributions

It is important to be informed of what these instructions do not tell you. Trustees, generally, do not withhold state and/or local income taxes from your retirement distributions. It is administratively too burdensome, inasmuch as disributees may live in any of the 50 different U.S. states. Such withholdings require extra paperwork and tax forms for forwarding the withholdings to each state's revenue department. Only for those plans distributed to thousands of retirees annually, do the trustees even consider state/local withholdings. In the great majority of cases, the state/local withholding boxes on Form 1099-R are left blank.

7

SOCIAL SECURITY OPTIONS

Your "Full Benefits" Age Is Set By Law At 65 Until Year 1999, After Which It Increases To 67. Applying for Benefits At Age 62 Gives You 80% Of Full Benefits Whereas, At 70, You Get About 130%. If You Work Between 62 And 70, You Will Lose Some Benefits ($1 For $2 Under 65; $1 For $3 Under 70). PLUS You Will Pay Income Taxes On Those Benefits. If At Tier 1 Level ($25,00/$32,000), 50% Are Taxable; If At Tier 2 ($34,000/$44,000), 85% Are Taxable. Tier 2 Levels Encroach On DOUBLE TAXATION Because You've Already Paid Social Security/Medicare Taxes On 50% Of ALL Contributions During Your Working-Life Years.

Not every occupationally active person is a participant in an employer-sponsored or self-sponsored retirement plan. But every such person **is** a participant in the Social Security System. He is a compulsory participant whether he wants to be or not. He is compelled to pay money (social security and medicare **taxes**) in. Yet, oddly, he is not compelled to take money out.

There is no statutory requirement that benefits be paid automatically to eligible-age participants. After being compelled to contribute over his (or her) working years, one must *apply* for benefits in his (or her) own name and Tax ID. It is in this application-for-benefits domain where the options lie.

The age at which one can apply for benefits ranges from as early as 62 to as late as 70 . . . even later. The common mistake that most eligible-age participants make is that, upon attaining age 62, they automatically apply for benefits. This forces them into a lower standard of retirement living than they may have contemplated. At such age, one's social security benefits are approximately 35% of his indexed-average income over his working life. As pointed out in Chapter 1, every retiree needs approximately 70% of his pre-retirement income, in order to enjoy properly his retirement years. Thus, clearly, social security is **not** a source of retirement income, in and of itself. It is a *supplement* to other sources of such income.

Once you recognize this fact (that social security is only a supplemental source of income), the options you have take on greater decision-making significance. After applying for benefits, do you continue to work full-time, part-time, or not at all? If you continue to work, will your benefits increase? If you continue to work, will you still be compelled to pay social security/medicare taxes? Are you prepared for the income taxes that you will pay on your benefits? And, what about your spouse (or ex-spouse): Does she (or he) have to apply when you do? Here, too, there are options to be considered.

Full Benefits Age

Ever since the inception of the social security system (in the mid-1930s), the benefit payments have been predicated upon the statutory age of 65. This is called the "full benefits age." This is the age at which your maximum benefits accrue, and for which a complex benefits formula has been devised. Anyone applying before this age would receive reduced benefits; anyone applying after this age would receive certain "credits" that would increase his benefits. The insurance intent was to have all benefit calculations referenced to the one age of 65.

Prior to 1984, all social security benefits were tax exempt to the recipients. That is, it was not regarded as tax accountable income (federal or state) in any way. It did not even have to be listed on one's annual tax return. This one feature alone eliminated many of the application options that one must consider today. Most applicants opted for age 65 for maximum benefit reasons.

In 1983 — on April 20, 1983 to be exact — a brainstorm hit Congress, the IRS, and the SSA (Social Security Administration).

As a way of "saving" the social security system from bankruptcy, why not tax "wealthy" recipients by applying a *means testing* formula? And, so, the '83 Act was hurriedly passed. This was just five days after the statutory due date of April 15th for filing regular income tax returns by individuals. There was no chance to complain: the die already had been cast.

The '83 Act contained another sleeper which few persons knew about until it was too late. It increased the statutory full benefits age from 65 to 67. This was done incrementally over a 22-year period commencing with the year 2000.

Persons born in 1937 or earlier are "grandfathered" in to receive full benefits (upon application) at age 65. Persons born in 1938 and later years have to wait longer than age 65 to reach full benefits eligibility. Just how long each person has to wait is tabulated in Figure 7.1. The data in Figure 7.1 is taken from the official SSA Publication No. 05-10035: *Retirement*. As you can see, year 2000 is the full benefits age turning point.

Meanwhile, all persons receiving social security benefits in 1984 and subsequent years have to report the benefit amounts on their tax returns annually. There is no grandfathering of the tax exempt status for those who applied for benefits prior to 1984. Thus, the '83 Act changed forever the options that one must consider before applying for his (or her) social security benefits. When one pays income tax on his social security benefits, he obviously receives less than full benefits for his statutory age. The SSA ducks this issue by referring all complaining inquiries to the IRS.

Complex Formula for Benefits

We are not going to pretend to tell you how to compute your benefits in order for you to decide at what age it is best for you to apply for them. In the first place, the formula that the SSA uses is very complex. In the second place, when you apply for benefits, much depends on your other sources of tax accountable income, and the tax consequences you may endure. Nevertheless, we do want you to know some of the factors that go into the formula.

All benefit computations are based upon an applicant being "fully insured" at age 62. This generally means your having worked

If You Were Born In -	You Will Be Age 62 in -	Your Age for Full Benefits is -
1937 or earlier	1999 or earlier	65 yrs
1938	2000	65 yrs, 2 mos
1939	2001	65 yrs, 4 mos
1940	2002	65 yrs, 6 mos
1941	2003	65 yrs, 8 mos
1942	2004	65 yrs, 10 mos
1943 - 1954	2005 - 2016	66 yrs
1955	2017	66 yrs, 2 mos
1956	2018	66 yrs, 2 mos
1957	2019	66 yrs, 2 mos
1958	2020	66 yrs, 2 mos
1959	2021	66 yrs, 2 mos
1960	2022	67 yrs

Fig. 7.1 - Post-1999 Increases in "Full Benefits" Age

a minimum of 40 quarters (or 10 full years) where you were compelled to pay social security/medicare taxes. Then, commencing with 1951 for persons born before 1930 or at age 22 if born in 1930 or later, your year-by-year earnings record is reconstructed and analyzed. Your earnings are compared with the national average earnings of all workers over the same period of contributory time. This comparison is used to arrive at an *Average Indexed Monthly Earnings* (AIME) for your account. The SSA has kept track of all workers' earnings since 1951 and has its own computer program for figuring your AIME up until you reach age 60. After age 60, your actual earnings are used. There is always a "2-year lag" in the posting of national statistics on worker earnings.

Once your AIME is determined for your first eligible year of application (at age 62), it is converted to a *Primary Insurance Amount* (PIA). The PIA applies a "social biasing factor" by adding to the AIME the following (*approximate*) amounts:

- 90% of the first $420 or less of AIME
- 32% of any AIME above $420 to $2,200
- 15% of any AIME above $2,200

Note that we indicate, parenthetically, the PIA conversions are "approximate." This is because the '83 Act added other sleepers to change the biasing factors so that persons earning $25,000 annually or less would get in benefits approximately 50% of their AIME. The PIA target for persons whose AIME was more than $25,000 annually, but less than $50,000, would be 40% of their AIME. The PIA target for persons earning more than $50,000 annually would be 30% of their AIME. Again, all of these amounts are approximate.

The whole idea of the '83 Act was to convert the social security system from a benefits insurance program to a benefits means testing program. This adds a punitive twist. Those who have planned and prepared in advance for their retirement independent of social security are being punished for doing so.

All PIAs are computed as of age 62. They are projected forward to age 65 as full benefits. Persons applying after, or working after, age 62 are awarded COLA (cost-of-living) and other adjustments based on their actual earnings. All adjustments result in a "rounding down" to the next lower monthly dollar amount.

Official Estimate Requests

The SSA has devised a quite simple form for requesting official estimates of your social security benefits. This form is titled: *Request for Earnings and Benefit Estimate Statement.* Look in your phone directory and jot down the toll-free 800-number for Social Security. Call that number and request a copy of the "benefit estimate" form. If you are married, get a copy for your spouse also. Benefit estimates are based on each worker's own earnings independent of his/her spouse.

The form asks for your social security (Tax ID) number, the date of your birth, your sex, your actual earnings for the past year, your estimated earnings for the current year, and the age at which you plan to apply for benefits (the form says: *Show only one age*). You are instructed to allow up to six weeks for a response.

Our suggestions is that you not request an official estimate until you have attained at least age 60. As mentioned above, age 60 is the latest posting age for establishing your AIME (average indexed monthly earnings). From 60 on, statistical indexing does not apply. After 60, your actual and estimated earnings are used.

We also suggest that you fill out a separate benefits estimate form for each of five years in a row: at age 61, 62, 63, 64, and 65. If you plan on continuing to work after 65, make separate similar requests for the next five years: at 66, 67, 68, 69, and 70. What you are trying to do is to determine the relative increase in benefits, as you defer applying for them past 62 or past 65. There are minimal — virtually insignificant — increases in benefits if you apply after age 70.

No matter at what age (62 to 70) you plan to formally apply for benefits, your PIA (primary insurance amount) will be based on your highest 35 years of actual earnings. Therefore, working past age 62 (if you are not otherwise forced into retirement) makes economic sense. You can enjoy a higher standard of living *without* applying for your benefits. As you'll see later below, collecting benefits while working or cashing-in on your investments, plus the higher taxes you'll pay, will not improve your retirement-age lifestyle. Collecting any social security may turn out to be a disappointment.

Application Age Comparisons

Formal application for benefits is quite easy these days. It is made by *teleclaim* (over the phone). An SSA employee fills out the form for you (titled: *Application for Retirement Insurance Benefits*), then mails it to you for signature. After signing it, you are allowed up to 60 days to withdraw your application. Thereafter, you are locked into the system . . . until you die.

It is important, therefore, that you select your application age with care. Do not be rushed into applying early simply because you'll be collecting benefits over a longer period of time. The benefit formula is figured in such a way that you'll receive approximately the same total lifetime benefits whether you apply at age 62, 65, or 70. If you apply at age 62, you'll get about 80% of your full benefits at 65. If you apply at age 70, you'll get about 130% of your age 65 benefits. Let's put these benefit features in perspective.

Back in Figure 1.4 we gave you a digest of IRS life expectancy tables, based on your current age of 50 on. Since we don't know your current age, we are going to assume that you are going to live to age 85. For quick comparison purposes, we are also going to assume that your PIA is $1,000 per month. Thus, if you apply at age 62 your PIA would be $800; at age 70, it would be $1,300. Assuming that you stop working altogether at age 62, let's compare your total lifetime benefits that you'll receive to age 85. The comparison is—

Age 62: $800/mo x 12 mo/yr x 23 yrs (85-62) = $220,000
Age 65: $1,000/mo x 12 mo/yr x 20 yrs (85-65) = $240,000
Age 70: $1,300/mo x 12 mo/yr x 15 yrs (85-70) = $234,000

On the assumptions above, there isn't much difference in the total lifetime benefits you receive, regardless of the age at which you apply for them. Get your own benefit estimates from the SSA, use Figure 1.4 for your life expectancy, and work out the numbers for yourself. You'll find that there isn't really too much difference. So, don't be pushed into applying prematurely for your benefits.

If you work past age 62 before applying, your PIAs will increase somewhat. This is because you will be paying social security/medicare taxes into the system; this is bound to increase your PIA amounts (to some extent). The best reason for working past age 62, without collecting benefits, is to enjoy a higher standard of living. However, apply for benefits no later than age 70, even if you continue working after that age. The reason is apparent below.

Working After Benefits Start

If you apply for benefits at age 70, and work past age 70, there is no reduction in your benefits. But, if you are collecting benefits and work between the ages of 62 and 70, you will lose some of those benefits. It's the law! It's all part of the social engineering trend that the '83 Act accelerated.

If you are collecting benefits, working, and under age 65, you will lose $1 in benefits for every $2 that you earn over (approximately) $8,000 per year. If collecting benefits, working, and over 65 (but under 70), you will lose $1 for every $3 you earn over (approximately) $11,000 per year. We say "approximately" because these earnings thresholds change with COLA and other adjustments, year after year.

To illustrate the effect of the loss in benefits, suppose you continue to work and earn $35,000 annually. You are under 65 and are collecting $900 monthly from SSA. That's $10,800 per year in benefits ($900/mo x 12 mo/yr). Your loss in benefits would be [35,000 − 8,000] x 1/2 = $13,500. This would wipe out all of your benefits entirely. But, isn't it better to collect $35,000 and pay tax on it, than try to live on $18,800 (10,800 benefits + 8,000 earnings) while still paying tax on your earnings?

Suppose you are earning the same $35,000 above, but are over 65 (under 70) and collecting $1,100 monthly from SSA ($13,200 per year). Now what is your loss in benefits?

Answer: [35,000 − 11,000] x 1/3 = $8,000. Thus, you will net $5,200 (13,200 − 8,000) out of the deal. It should come as no surprise that the $5,200 is NOT free of income tax. Your net-net benefits are more likely to be around $4,000 or less. The taxation of social security benefits certainly puts a damper on the worthwhileness of said benefits. We'll tell you more about the taxation process below.

When you lose benefits as a consequence of working between the ages of 62 and 70, you don't lose them in the same year that you collect them. You lose them in the *following* year. This means that you wind up paying tax on the full benefits in the year received. The sad irony is: You get no tax refund the following year for the loss in benefits.

Our message is this. If you are over 62 but under 70 and earning $35,000 or more per year, we see no point in applying for and collecting your social security benefits. It's just too much of a hassle. The hassle will go on year after year, with the SSA recomputing your net benefits to lower amounts, while simultaneously the IRS taxes you on the higher PIA amounts. If you earn less than $35,000 or cease working altogether, then by all means apply for your benefits at that time. In some cases, you can make the application retroactive back six months. Talk to the SSA teleclaim representative about this.

SSA to IRS: Form 1099

When you start collecting benefits, regardless of age, who — what government bureaucracy — is the first to know about it besides you? It's your favorite: the IRS, of course. What the government giveth with one hand, it taketh away from you with the other. The SSA and IRS work hand-in-hand in this regard.

At the end of each benefits collection year, the SSA totals the amount of payments made to you. It then subtracts from this total any benefits *repaid* that are credited to the current year (due to earnings thresholds and other adjustments from the previous year). The net amount for the current year is then reported to the IRS.

The SSA report to the IRS is made on Form SSA-1099: *Social Security Benefit Statement.* This form consists of 7 boxes of information, as depicted in Figure 7.2. It is Box 5: Net Benefits, that the IRS computer sees. The Box 5 amount with your name and Tax ID (social security number) goes to the IRS electronically. A hard copy of the entire form goes to you for your records. If your spouse is also collecting benefits, she (or he) too will get a separate Form SSA-1099, with its Box 5 amount also going to the IRS.

Why do you suppose the IRS is in on the deal? Answer: It wants to tax you (and your spouse) on your social benefits. The IRS's taxing *includes* any and all medicare insurance premiums that were deducted by the SSA from your monthly benefits.

Under current law, social security benefits are **not** subject to withholdings like other payers to you of compensation, interest, dividends, pensions, annuities, etc. But a change in policy is being considered if you expressly request withholdings from your benefits. The SSA now does this if you retire to a foreign country.

Because your benefits are not subject to withholdings, the IRS watches the Box 5 information in its Big Computer like a hawk. It also takes a sudden interest in any tax exempt interest you may receive. Similarly for your IRA distributions, your pensions and annuities, and other forms of nonemployee compensation from which no withholdings have been made. All of a sudden, now, you are tax suspect. Especially so if you are classed as a "wealthy retiree."

FORM SSA - 1099	SOCIAL SECURITY BENEFIT STATEMENT	
Year	● Part of Your Benefits May Be Taxable Income ● See Reverse Side for More Information	
Box 1 - Your Name	Box 2 - Your SSN (Tax ID)	
Box 3 - Benefits Paid $ _____	Box 4 - Benefits Repaid $ _____	**Box 5 - Net Benefits** $ _____
Description of Amount in Box 3 ● ● ● ●	Description of Amount in Box 4 ● ●	
	Box 6 - Your Address	
	Box 7 - Your SSA Claim No. _____	

Fig. 7.2 - General Contents of Form SSA-1099

Two Tiers of Retirement Wealth

With its success in social engineering, the '83 Act made a major change in the purpose of social security. It created the first-tier definition of a wealthy retiree. A single person whose combined income (earned and unearned) exceeds $25,000 while collecting social security is prima facie deemed to be wealthy. A married couple filing jointly whose combined income exceeds $32,000 (while one or both are collecting social security) is also deemed wealthy. And wealthy persons — whether retired or not — always have to be taxed more than unwealthy persons.

Gloating over their success with the '83 Act, Congress and the IRS in 1993 put another one over on wealthy retirees. The obfuscating "Omnibus Reconciliation Act of 1993" was enacted. This '93 Act established a second-tier definition of retirement wealth: superwealthy retirees. This class gathers in all those collecting social security benefits with other combined incomes exceeding $34,000 single, and $44,000 married filing jointly. These "Tier 2" retirees, as they are now known, have a higher percentage of social security benefits taxed than do "Tier 1" retirees.

In a nutshell, Tier 1 retirees — the ordinary wealthy ones — have 50% of their social benefits taxed. Tier 2 — the superwealthy ones — have 85% of their benefits taxed. In both cases, the actual tax rates that are applied depend on other sources of income, whether taxed or not. Here is where tax-exempt interest income now takes on a conspicuous role by being required to be displayed on every retiree's Form 1040. Prior to the '83 and '93 Acts, tax-exempt interest never had to be reported on tax returns.

Tier 1 and Tier 2 retirees have their feet anchored in concrete. It's there in Section 86 of the Internal Revenue Code. The short title of this section is: Social Security Benefits. The correct title really should be: **Taxation of** *Social Security Benefits*. Nothing appears in the IR Code unless it is subject to tax. Everyone knows this. So, why do Congress and the IRS try to soft-pedal the hard, cold, truth of their Acts?

Overview of IRC Sec. 86

Section 86: (Taxation of) Social Security Benefits, consists of approximately 2,000 words. It is arranged into six primary subsections, namely:

(a) In General
(b) Taxpayers to Whom (a) Applies
(c) Base Amount and Adjusted Amount
(d) Social Security (and Railroad Retirement)
(e) Limitation (Re) Lump-Sum Payment
(f) Treatment as Pension or Annuity

Our focus at this point is on subsections (a), (b), and (c).

Subsection 86(a) has two principal paragraphs: (1) base amount, and (2) additional amount. These two paragraphs read in essential part as—

*86(a)(1) — Except as provided in paragraph (2), gross income for the taxable year of any taxpayer . . . includes social security benefits in an amount equal to the **lesser of**—*

> *(A) one-half of the social security benefits received during the taxable year, **or***
> *(B) one-half of the excess described in subsection (b)(1)* [relating to "modified" adjusted gross income].

> *86(a)(2) — In the case of a taxpayer* [who] *. . . exceeds the adjusted base amount, the amount included in gross income . . . shall be . . . the **lesser of**—*

> *(A) the sum of (i) 85 percent of such excess, plus (ii) an amount equal to one-half of the difference between the adjusted base amount and the base amount of the taxpayer, **or***
> *(B) 85 percent of the social security benefits received during the taxable year.*

Correspondingly, subsection (c) has paragraphs (1) and (2). Its paragraph (1) sets the "base amount" at $25,000 single and $32,000 married filing jointly. Its paragraph (2) sets the "adjusted base amount" (additional amount) at $34,000 single and $44,000 married filing jointly.

Paragraph (1) of subsections (a) and (c) establishes the Tier 1 wealth class mentioned previously, whereas paragraph (2) of the same subsections establishes the Tier 2 wealth class.

Actually, subsection (c), paragraphs (1)(C) and 2(C) establishes a third wealth class: married taxpayers who file separately, yet who live together one day or more during the taxable year. Their wealth threshold is **zero**. If each spouse lives apart from the other *at all times during the taxable year*, each is treated as a single taxpayer whereby the Tier 1 and Tier 2 thresholds apply.

Are you beginning to see now the lengths that Congress and the IRS will go to, to confuse retirees who are collecting their social security benefits? There's still more.

"Modified" Adjusted Gross Income

The real chicanery comes when we tell you what income you must include when establishing your retirement wealth (for the thresholds above). For this, subsection 86(b)(2) is a masterpiece of taxation double-talk. As paraphrased, 86(b)(2) says that your *modified* adjusted gross income (for social security taxing) comprises the **sum of**—

1. Your regular adjusted gross income (without regard to social security),
2. Income from U.S. savings bonds used to pay higher education tuition and fees (normally excludable),
3. Personal service income earned while residing abroad (normally excludable up to $70,000),
4. Income from sources within Guam, American Samoa, Mariana Islands, and Puerto Rico (normally excludable), and
5. Interest on municipal bonds received or accrued . . . *during the taxable year which is exempt from tax.*

In other words, the IRS has found a backdoor way to tax otherwise excludable/exempt income through your social security benefits. Once you collect any amount of social security, you expose much of your nontaxable, excludable, and exempt income to the Tier 1 and Tier 2 wealth tests.

A few brave retirees have challenged this encroachment on our too-few tax freedoms. The judicial rationale that is used to uphold this encroachment is convoluted, to say the least. Three selected court cases will illustrate the convolution.

In *P. Shapiro*, DC N.J., 86-2 USTC ¶ 9817, 646 FSupp 1127, the court held—

Inclusion of tax-exempt interest in addition to social security benefits, in determining the taxpayer's gross income under Code Sec. 86, did not violate the principle of intergovernmental tax immunity. The tax was not directly imposed on the exempt interest.

In *L.G. Boli*, CA-FC, 87-2 USTC ¶ 9566, 831 F2d 276, the court held—

Inclusion of tax-exempt interest in the calculation of a couple's modified adjusted gross income did not result in an impermissible tax on their tax-exempt interest. The narrow impact of the formula under Code Sec. 86 determined only the portion of social security benefits that was includible in [their] gross income. The increased tax that resulted . . . was a tax upon their benefits, not [upon] their tax-exempt interest.

In *B. Levine*, 64 TCM 531, Dec. 48,430(M), TC Memo 1992-469, the court held—

Including a portion of the taxpayer's social security payments in his taxable income did not result in double taxation, nor was it unconstitutional to take tax-exempt interest earned on state bonds into account in determining the amount of social security payments included in [taxable] income.

All three cases above touch the nerve of "double taxation" (social security taxes paid on earnings plus income taxes paid on social security benefits). The courts passed over this matter too lightly.

In still another case: *O.Q. Foust*, 70 TCM Dec. 50,994 (M), TC Memo 1995-536, the court upheld the IRS's position that it could retroactively tax social security benefits, if there were increases in taxable income resulting from deficiencies determined by the IRS. There is just no escaping the social security tax ax.

Read Your Form 1040 Instructions

When the SSA sends your social security benefits information to the IRS, it also tries to alert you that "part of your benefits may be taxable." It does this on the back of Form SSA-1099 that is sent to you. There is a little worksheet there that is designed to make you aware of the Tier 1 and Tier 2 threshold levels. After this awareness, the SSA instructions say—

See Social Security Benefits in your Federal income tax return instructions.

The Form 1040 (or 1040A) instructions are quite confusing. Right off, the instructions address tier 1 and tier 2 *railroad retirement* benefits which have no relationship whatsoever to the Tier 1 and Tier 2 wealth thresholds for the taxation of social security benefits. You are also told that, if you received railroad retirement benefits treated as social security, you should receive a Form RRB-1099. The amounts on Form RRB-1099 are to be entered on Form 1040/1040A at the line for "Pensions and annuities" and **not** on the line for "Social security benefits." See our Figure 7.3 for the location distinction between these two different entries.

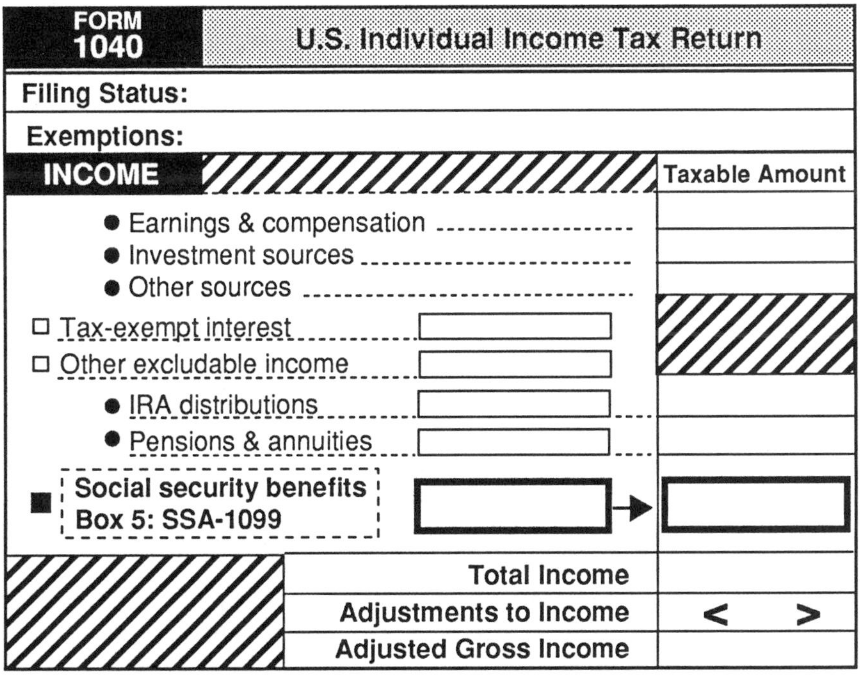

Fig. 7.3 - Your Social Security Benefit Lines on Form 1040

As if the above were not confusing enough, the instructions tell you to prepare your return initially, without regard to your social security benefits. This produces your regular/ordinary "adjusted gross income." Then you enter your Box 5 (Form SSA-1099) benefits in the left-hand offset space shown in Figure 7.3. Next, the instructions tell you to use the accompanying worksheet to compute the taxable portion of your benefits, or to use the worksheet(s) in Publication 915, whichever are applicable.

Frankly, we think the IRS social security worksheets are illiterate. They are prepared by young accountants and attorneys (in their 30s) who have no concept of what retirement-age taxpayers go through. Nevertheless, the substance of these worksheets is as follows:

(1) Your ordinary adjusted gross income _____

(2) **Plus** tax-exempt interest and other previously specified excludable income _____

(3) Modified adjusted gross income: (1) + (2) _____

(4) **Plus** 50% of social security benefits _____

(5) Provisional income: (3) + (4) _____

(6) **Less**
• Tier 1 threshold, if (5) less than Tier 2; *otherwise* Tier 2 _____

(7) Excess over threshold: (5) – (6) _____

(8) • If Tier 1, multiply (7) by 50% ----------------
• If Tier 2, multiply (7) by 85% ----------------

(9) LESSER of (7) or (8) _____

Item (9) is the amount of your social security benefits that is taxable. Enter on Form 1040/1040A at the line designated as *Social security benefits*: **Taxable amount.**

If all of the above is too much for you, or if the IRS worksheets are too confusing, we offer a simple approach that you can use. If your modified adjusted gross income (MAGI) is less than the Tier 1 threshold (25,000/32,000), enter "zero" as your taxable amount. If your MAGI is greater than Tier 1 but less than Tier 2 (34,000/44,000), enter 50% of your benefits as taxable. If your MAGI is greater than Tier 2, enter 85% of your benefits as taxable. Presumably, the IRS will correct your entries if any errors have been made.

8

HOME EQUITY CONVERSION

Over Your Entire Working Lifespan, You Can Build Up A Substantial Equity (VALUE MINUS DEBT) In Your Home. As A Supplement To Other Income, There Is Desire To Convert And Consume This Equity Prudently. Your Options Are: (1) Sell Outright (Cash Or Installment) And Move To A Lower Cost Home; (2) Stay In Your Home By Borrowing Against Your Equity (Via RML Or HEL: See Text); (3) Stay Put, But Sell Part With RETAINED LIFE ESTATE; Or, (4) Sell/Exchange Into A LIFE CARE FACILITY Sponsored By A "Charitable Remainder" Organization. Upon Sale, You May Claim The New $500,000 Exclusion Of Gain.

If you have been employed or self-employed regularly throughout your working life, you probably have bought and sold a number of homes (primary residences). Typically, the average worker occupies from five to eight homes up to the time he is ready to retire. How many homes have you sold and replaced throughout your 30- to 50-year working career?

If you have taken advantage of the special *rollover of gain* tax rules when acquiring your replacement residences, you could have — should have — built up a substantial capital gain equity in your home. How do you convert this equity into fulfilling your old-age and medicare needs? Do you sell outright, or do you stay put and pursue other options?

The term "equity" means market value (what your home would sell for) minus indebtedness (what your outstanding mortgage is).

Most persons approaching retirement try to get their mortgage paid way down. When they do retire, their mortgage payments, if any, are a small percentage of their lower amount of retirement income. As a consequence, for persons approaching or just entering retirement, the equity in their home is usually quite substantial — often between $150,000 and $600,000 . . . or more.

What you do or can do about this equity is what this chapter is all about. Do you stay in your home; do you sell it; do you "reverse mortgage" it; do you "life estate" it; do you exchange it for a life care facility? What do you do?

Common Mistakes Made

It is not uncommon for some retirement age persons to have an equity of between $150,000 and $600,000 in their last working home. With so much equity (money) tied up in a personal residence, there is a burning desire to get the money out and "do something" with it. "It's idle money," you say to yourself. "Why not put it to better use immediately upon retirement?" Doing so with a "burning desire" often leads to costly mistakes.

The most common mistake is the selling of one's home simultaneously with retirement, or doing so shortly before or shortly after. There are too many other important decisions to make at about the same time. Yet, many retirees rush to sell their high equity home and move to a lower cost area where they buy a cheaper replacement residence. They pay cash for the new home and use the excess proceeds from the sale for other purposes.

Some of these other uses of the equity money are—

- Investing in various types of mutual funds.
- Placement in variable annuities for later withdrawal.
- Loans and gifts to children and relatives.
- Loans and gifts to churches and charities.
- Speculative ventures, hoping to make more money.
- Gambling, vacation, and recreational activities.

We know of one retiree (surviving spouse) who sold her home, bought a small apartment in a retirement complex, and still had about $250,000 left over. Her financial counselor (a female) urged that she put $50,000 into each of five different limited partnerships . . . to spread the risk. Within a few years, three of the partnerships went bankrupt; one lost money but dissolved and returned $30,000; the other broke even financially. Distressed by the bankruptcies, the retiree sold her interest to another partner for a 20% discount (thereby losing another $10,000). Altogether, she recovered $70,000 on her $250,000 excess home equity money.

We know of one retired couple who sold their home (before August 5, 1997) and netted $185,000 cash from the proceeds. Since they had two years to acquire a replacement residence to avoid some of the tax on their capital gains, they decided to go on a vacation and gambling spree. In just over a year's time, they lost the entire $185,000! They had nothing left to pay the capital gains tax, let alone get a replacement residence. They had to apply to the IRS for "hardship relief" (via Form 911).

We know of another retirement-age couple who got divorced. They agreed to sell their home and split the proceeds. The selling price was $580,000 of which $330,000 was cumulative capital gain. Shortly after the divorce, the husband was in an automobile accident and totally disabled. He spent all of his share of the capital gain money on hospital care, doctors' bills, and special nursing. Because he and his ex-wife failed to report the sale on their tax return, the IRS sent the husband a demand notice for $162,000 in tax . . . *plus* $41,000 in penalties.

All of the above are real-life examples of that "burning desire" to do something with that equity money sitting idle in one's home. Our recommendation is this: Do not make any decisions regarding the equity in your home for at least two years after you retire. Use this time to adjust to a retirement lifestyle. Then when you decide to convert your equity, your judgment will be more sound.

Supplement to Social Security

Sound judgment is fostered by treating your home equity as a *supplement* to your social security benefits. As pointed out in Chapter 7, the social security system is not designed to be your sole source of retirement income. It, itself, is a supplement to more ordinary sources of retirement income, such as employer plans, IRA distributions, savings and investments, part-time working, and other. The term "and other" includes the equity in your home plus any last-resort savings/investments you may have.

Let's put your home equity in perspective with your lifetime social security benefits. For this, consider that you and your spouse are each 65 years old. Assume further that your combined, indexed lifetime earnings averaged $35,000 per year. (This is purely an assumption for illustration purposes.) Your approximate (husband and wife) monthly social security benefits would be $1,600. If you both lived to age 85 — our basic assumption throughout this book — your lifetime social security benefits would approximate $385,000 ($1,600/mo x 12 mo/yr x 20 yrs).

With a home equity nest-egg of between $150,000 and $600,000 (as postulated above), your home equity money is certainly on a par with your lifetime social security benefits. Think of it, if you will, as your backup security money, should the social security system fail. Therefore, it seems, to us at least, that you'd want to preserve your home equity money and spread its conversion/consumption out over your actuarially remaining lifetime. Obviously, you don't want to blow it, as the prior examples have illustrated.

There are a number of options you can pursue for conservatively converting/consuming your home equity money. Which option you pursue depends on your state of health, the presence of a spouse (if any), and on how long you intend to remain in your home after you retire from working.

Reconstruct Your Tax Records

No matter how you convert your home equity, any transaction you undertake will involve *tax accounting*. There is no escaping this fact. This is because your home is tax treated as a "capital asset." The term "capital," of course, means money. Any transaction involving a capital asset is electronically reported to the IRS. In the case of your home, the reporting is done on **Form 1099-S**: *Proceeds from Real Estate Transactions*. The reporting is done by the intermediary responsible for the legal technicalities of the transaction under state law where your home is located. Form 1099-S requires that the **gross proceeds** be reported, even though you might not sell or exchange your home outright at the time. This gives the IRS an amount to tax attack in the event you fail to report the transaction on your year-of-conversion tax return.

For *each home* that you sold throughout your working life, you were supposed to complete **Form 2119**: *Sale of Your Home*, and attach it to your year-of-sale tax return. Have you done this consistently over your pre-retirement homeselling life? If not, you have the serious job of reconstructing your records ahead of you. This is one reason why we suggested waiting two years before making any irreversible home equity decisions. It takes time to reconstruct a lifetime of home ownership records.

If you have sold and replaced five to eight homes in your 30- to 50-year working lifetime, as we have postulated previously, you should have five to eight Forms 2119 in your permanent tax records. Do you have them? Probably not. If you have prepared said forms consistently over the years, the very least that the IRS expects of you is that you have Form 2119 for the last prior sale for which your current home is the replacement.

Why is Form 2119 on your last prior sale so important?

Because the last two lines on Form 2119 tell the IRS the cumulative history of all your prior homes owned and sold. The last line is the initial *adjusted basis* of your current home; the next-to-last line is the *postponed gain* on all of your prior homes on which you have not paid tax (due to the special rule on homesale "rollovers"). Just because you have — or soon will be — retired, your cumulative postponed gain is not forgiven. You still have to tax account for it when you sell, exchange, or otherwise convert the equity in your current home.

When you do so, you first have to establish the market gain, if any, on your current home. You start with the initial adjusted basis on the last line of your last prior Form 2119, then add any improvements that you have made since occupancy. Then follow the procedure in the upper portion of Form 2119 for your current transaction. The challenge that you face is depicted for you in Figure 8.1. Obviously, you need accurate backup records to properly complete Form 2119.

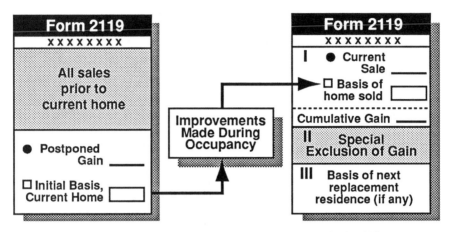

Fig. 8.1 - Tax Records Importance of Form 2119: Sale of Home

Editorial Note: As of August 5, 1997, sales of residences with a gross sales price of $500,000 or less ($250,000 or less in the case of a single person) are not reported to the IRS on Form 1099-S.

The Former $125,000 Exclusion

If you had done your homework properly (before August 5, 1997), there was a true retirement tax plum awaiting you. This was so provided in IRC Section 121. Its mouth-filling title was: *One-Time Exclusion of Gain from Sale of Principal Residence by Individual Who Has Attained Age 55*. This specified age 55 obviously meant that the one-time exclusion was intended to apply only to retirement-age persons.

Section 121 is an excellent example of how a tax law can be written clearly. Two subsections pertinent to our discussion are—

Sec. 121(a) **General Rule.**
At the election of the taxpayer, gross income does not include gain from the sale or exchange of property if—
(1) the taxpayer has attained the age of 55 before the date of such sale or exchange, and
(2) during the 5-year period ending on the date of the sale or exchange, such property has been owned and used by the

taxpayer as his principal residence for periods aggregating 3 years or more.

Sec. 121(b) **Limitations.**
(1) The amount of gain excluded from gross income under subsection (a) shall not exceed $125,000 ($62,500 in the case of a separate return by a married individual).

A $125,000 exclusion is a lot of capital gain (home equity) money that you don't have to pay tax on. At a nominal combined federal/state tax rate of 36%, say, the tax saving alone on this exclusion is $45,000 ($125,000 x 0.36). The entire $125,000 is equivalent to approximately $6^{1/2}$ years of nominal social security benefits (husband and wife).

The implication that we are making is that you should have saved your one-time exclusion until you are actually ready to retire. You should not have used it just because you are over age 55. In practice, many taxpayers have not heeded our advice on this point. They have probably missed out on better opportunities in tax years 1997 and thereafter.

The New $500,00 Exclusion

On August 5, 1997, Congress and the President chose to replace the former $125,000 exclusion with a $500,000 married persons exclusion, when selling one's primary residence. This new exclusion is generally allowed *each time* a residence is sold, after meeting certain eligibility requirements. The new exclusion is allowed no more frequently than once every two years. It is hard for us to imagine that any principal residence will appreciate in value up to $500,000 every two years. This poses the challenge of accumulating the gains until one is truly ready to retire.

To be eligible for the new exclusion-of-gain, you must have owned the residence and occupied it for at least two of the five years prior to its sale or exchange. In the case of joint filers not sharing a common principal residence, an exclusion of $250,000 is allowable on a qualifying sale by either of the two spouses. Once both spouses satisfy the eligibility rules, and two years have passed since the last exclusion was allowed to either of them, the taxpayers may subsequently exclude $500,000 of gain. Being over age 55 is no longer required.

The new $500,000 exclusion is prescribed by Section 121, as revised. The revised title is: *Exclusion of Gain From Sale of Principal Residence.* Its subsection (a) reads—

> *Gross income shall not include gain from the sale or exchange of property if, during the 5-year period ending on the date of the sale or exchange, such property has been owned and used by the taxpayer as the taxpayer's principal residence for periods aggregating 2 years or more.*

Altogether Section 121 consists of about 1,600 tax law words, of which we have quoted only 50 such words.

Subsection 121(f): *Election to Have Section Not Apply,* implies that homeowners can cumulatively save their gains up to $500,000. However, subsection (f) — consisting of just 23 words — is silent on this point. Presumably, IRS regulations will clarify the implication. Meanwhile, be informed that a $500,000 lump-sum nest egg at time of retirement would be equivalent to approximately 25 years of social security benefits.

Outright Sale Options

After two years of retirement or semi-retirement, you may decide to sell your home outright. You want a smaller place (condo or apartment) in a retirement-type community or near your children and grandchildren. The idea is that you will use some of the sale proceeds to get another place to live, then invest the rest. At this stage, your mortgage should be paid off or nearly so. If it is not paid off, pay it off before you make the sale. This way, you can become the new mortgage owner, should you want to.

For the year of sale, you must complete Form 2119 and attach it to that year's Form 1040 return. Part I of Form 2119 computes your overall gain on the sale, including all prior postponed gains. Part II of the form allows you to claim the $125,000/$500,000 exclusion mentioned above. Part III of the form is where you indicate your subsequent options.

After the sale is consummated, you have at least four options that you can pursue. These are:

(1) Pay the applicable federal/state tax on the gain less exclusion, and be done with your Form 2119 reporting.

(2) Wait no more than two years before deciding whether to get a replacement residence or to become a renter; to signify this "waiting," you must answer on Form 2119 the two replacement intent questions.

(3) Purchase a replacement residence, complete Form 2119, and keep a copy of the form until you subsequently sell/exchange that residence.

(4) Select the installment sale method for reporting the tax by attaching to Form 2119, **Form 6252**: *Installment Sale Income.*

We summarize these options for you in Figure 8.2.

If you decide not to buy a replacement residence, the net sale proceeds have to be further reduced by any applicable federal/state taxes. Once this is done, the remaining money — your after-tax equity — is yours to invest as you see fit. We urge care, prudence, and conservatism. Among your choices should be savings accounts, CDs, T-bills/notes, money market funds, growth-income mutual funds, tax-exempt muni bond funds, and similar.

If you decide to sell via the installment method, the investment of your excess proceeds is automatically done for you. This is because the installment method puts you in the position of being the mortgage lender to the new buyer. This time, you claim the mortgage interest as *income* — instead of an expense — on your tax return. Also reportable as income is a small portion of your capital gain (less the exclusion), which you compute each year on Form 6252: Installment Sale Income.

By all means, you be the *first* mortgagor: not the second or further down. Since you are of retirement age, you want your installment note secured by the real property in which you yourself once lived. Make it a "balloon payment" note with an "acceleration

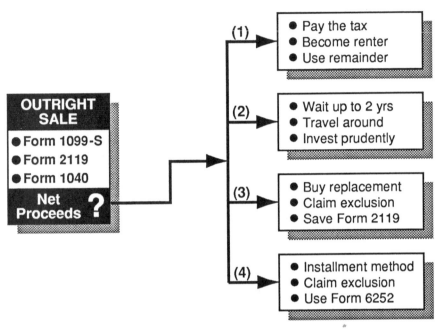

Fig. 8.2 - Options to Consider After Sale of Your Home

clause" (due in full on resale or refinancing). Amortize the note over 30 years, but make the balloon payment due in 5, 10, but no more than 15 years. Otherwise, you may not live long enough to see the note fully amortized.

Reverse Mortgage Loan (RML)

Not every retiree wants to sell his home and move to a new location. Many prefer to stay where they are until some overriding event (such as major illness, death of spouse, financial hardship) "forces" the sale. Yet they want access to the equity in their home to use for monthly expenditures as needed.

If you prefer staying in your home while tapping into your equity, a *reverse mortgage loan* could be the way to go. A number of nationally known insurance companies will actually lend you money against your equity. They do this in the form of monthly payments **made to you**. This is the reverse of your making payments to a mortgage lender. These reverse payments can range from $800 to $1,800 per month (or more) depending on the age at which you enter into an annuity-type contract. You pay nothing to the insurance lender until you sell or die. Meanwhile, the money you receive is not tax accountable. (It will be later.) If interested, contact a real estate agent or life insurance agent who is knowledgeable on the subject. Reverse mortgage loans (RMLs) are a relatively new product in the financial world.

Only companies with very large cash reserves — hundreds of millions of dollars or more — participate in RMLs. Even at this, they limit their commitment to each homeowner to a range of from $150,000 to $600,000. Unlike an ordinary mortgage which is advanced to you in one lump sum, which shrinks as you pay it back, a reverse mortgage is a debit account which starts at zero and grows and grows. The very first debits against an RML account are various setup fees: loan origination fees, broker finding fees, attorney fees, administrative fees, etc.

After your RML account is established, each payment of principal made to you is ADDED to your account. At the same time, a market rate of interest is also ADDED to your account. Before long, the compounding effect of the add-ons takes on a financial cycle of its own. There is interest on interest, interest on principal, interest on fees, and interest on any special draws you may make. (Some RML accounts provide check-writing privileges.)

After 5, 10, 15 years or so, the compounding of debt due becomes overwhelming. The monthly add-ons race out of proportion to the amount of principal payouts. It is for this reason that some states require independent RML counseling before it is legal for a retiree to sign an RML contract. One duty of the counselor is to provide guidance on when to get out of an RML. "Getting out" requires that you sell your home, pay off the compounded debt, and share any appreciation of your home with the lender.

Home Equity Loan (HEL)

If an RML is unpalatable to you, there is another approach: get a home equity loan. This type of loan — HEL — is very common these days, by young and old alike. As a retirement-age person you have an advantage. You are a better credit risk because your home is paid off or nearly so. The lender takes very little risk when you apply for an HEL amount less than 75% of the true equity in your home. Consequently, the setup fees are quite nominal.

An HEL loan does have to be paid back on a monthly basis. However, you can structure the arrangement as a *line of credit* rather than as a lump-sum take-out loan. In other words, you can draw on the loan regularly or irregularly as you need extra funds. This makes the arrangement a flexible "extra money" source while still living in your home.

Typically, HELs can be amortized over 20, 30 or 40 years. We suggest the longest amortized period that is offered to you. While you'll pay more total interest on the amount you have borrowed, you know full well that you are not going to take 30 to 40 years to pay back the loan.

Most taxpayers tend to sell their home within five to 15 years after full retirement. This is because they (usually) have a larger home then they need; their physical ability to take care of the home diminishes; and (often) they want a smaller place as an excuse to get rid of some of their furniture, furnishings, and collectibles that they have gathered over many working years. When the time comes to sell — as it inevitably will — you will have a balloon payback to make on your HEL loan.

For guidance purposes, a comparison of the features between an RML and an HEL is presented in Figure 8.3. Choose the one that you feel the most comfortable with. Either way, you can tap into your equity, use the money, and still live in your home until you decide to sell. Either way, also, there is a balloon settlement to be made with the lender.

Life Estate Sale

If making a large balloon payback at time of sale disturbs you, there is one near-ideal alternative that you can pursue. This is a life estate sale . . . or more properly, a sale *with retained life estate.* You stay in your home but you sell outright a portion called: "remainder interest."

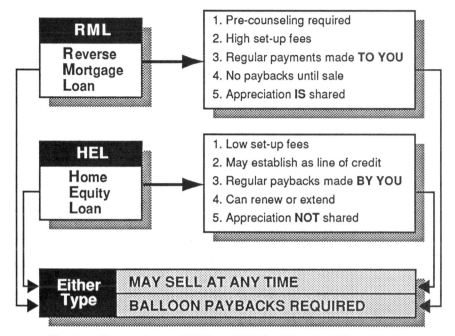

Fig. 8.3 - Comparison of RML vs. HEL for "Tapping" Your Equity

Think of your home, if you will, as two legally/actuarially separate pieces of property. One piece is a "life interest"; this is the piece that you retain. The other piece is designated as the "remainder interest"; this is the piece that you sell. Each piece is actuarially and statistically defined as a fraction to five decimal places. The two fractions must add up to 100%. For example, suppose the life interest fraction were 0.67972; the remainder interest fraction would be 0.32028 (0.67972 + 0.32028 = 1.00000).

IRC Section 7520: *Valuation Tables*, requires the IRS to publish every 10 years statistical tables which determine—

the value of any annuity, any interest for life or a term of years, or any remainder or reversionary interest.

The most recent tables were published in 1989 and are applicable through 1999. They are available to the public as **Publications 1457 and 1458**. They are complex and difficult to understand and use by persons who are not professional actuaries. But they are available.

Our point is that, for any given age, one's life interest and remainder interest in his home can be officially determined. Consequently, at any time during your retirement, you can decide to sell your remainder interest. For example, suppose at age 65 your remainder fraction is 0.32030. This means that you can sell 32% of your home, collect the money, and stay in it for the rest of your life. After the remainder sale, the property is re-titled as Tenants in Common: 68% yours, 32% the buyer's.

The problem with life estate sales is: Who's going to buy your remainder interest? From a buyer's point of view, it is "restricted title" property; it cannot be sold without your concurrence. As a result, such sales make sense only to close family members who are probably going to inherit the property anyway. It makes sense because the longer you live, the greater their remainder fraction grows . . . UNTAXED. Correspondingly, your life estate fraction diminishes . . . which reduces your tax accountability when you do sell or die.

Let's put this family benefit generalization into better perspective. At age 85, for example, your ownership interest would diminish from approximately 68% (at age 65) to approximately 35%. On the other hand, the family member who purchased the remainder interest for 32% of the fair market value of your home, would find that his ownership interest had grown to approximately 65%. Here's a case where both sides of the ownership coin derive a tax benefit. Check this with your own tax advisor.

Exchange for Life Care

If no family member is interested in buying the remainder portion of your home, there is yet another way to go. You can buy/exchange your equity into a life care facility. A life care facility is a retirement home complex sponsored by a religious, charitable, hospital, or fraternal organization. These entities, now well established as part of the lifestyle of gray American, offer a wide range of options to persons over age 62 for buying in, or exchanging into, a packaged program of care for life. The programs are most appealing to those approaching their "twilight years." The net effect is that one exchanges — or can exchange — the equity in his home for housing, medical care, and financial security . . . to the very end. We depict this idea in Figure 8.4.

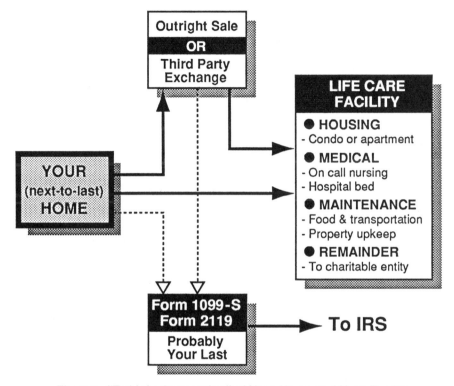

Fig. 8.4 - "Twilight Conversion" of Your Home and Your Equity

What makes life care programs viable is that the entities which sponsor them are *exempt* from tax. They are so because of Code Section 501(c)(3): ***Organizations Exempt from Taxation.*** The essence of this subsection is that—

An organization [which] *is organized and **operated exclusively** for . . . charitable,* [etc.] *purposes . . . shall be exempt from taxation . . .* [provided that] *no part of its net earnings inures to the benefit of any private shareholder or individual.* [Emphasis added.]

The idea behind a Section 501(c)(3) exempt organization is that, once an individual is accepted into its program, that individual cannot be subsequently discharged because of his or her mental, medical, or financial inabilities. This is a comforting thought for one's latter days.

Most life care arrangements require an entry fee (which is nonrefundable), a specified lump-sum payment amount (depending on the housing/hospital options), and a monthly maintenance fee (for food, transportation, upkeep of grounds, etc.). The entry fee and lump-sum payment constitute the equivalent of purchasing a replacement residence. When the sale/exchange of your home is life-care consummated, you prepare perhaps your last Form 2119. After claiming your $125,000 exclusion of gain on sales prior to August 5, 1997, or your $250,000/$500/000 exclusion of gain on sales after August 5, 1997, any remainder portion is deeded to the charitable organization. This way, you pay no death tax on the *charitable remainder* portion. And, if the title deed was prepared in accordance with the IRS's remainder interest tables, you could actually get a charitable deduction on your Form 1040 return while you are alive. This is the ultimate conversion of your home equity.

9

MEDICAL EXPENDITURES

Major Medical Expenses Are Allowable Deductions On Schedule A Of Your Form 1040 Tax Return. Before Any "Bottom Line" Tax Savings Accrue, THREE SUBTRACTIONS Are Made, Namely: (1) Insurance Reimbursement, (2) 7.5% AGI, And (3) The Standard Deduction. At Age 65, You Are Eligible For Medicare A; You Paid Taxes For Its Hospital Coverage (Excluding Doctors) Throughout Your Working Years. Medicare B And Its Supplements — Which You Pay For Separately — Cover Limited Medical Services, Including Long-Term Care. A Durable Power Of Attorney Becomes "Pull-The-Plug" Insurance Against Financial Ruin.

At all stages of life, there are ups and downs. And so it is in retirement. The difference is that the downs tend to become more so as the retirement years roll by. This is particularly true of medical expenditures; they definitely increase as your age increases. It is just that ye old body cells, bones, and muscles are not young and vibrant any more.

Contrary to the perception of many occupationally active persons, not all retirees are elderly, decrepit, and dysfunctional. Many retirees — the majority in fact — have an active ongoing life relatively free of major medical concerns. Nevertheless, one has to prepare for and decide on how to handle large expenditures should the need arise. This suggests the prudence of setting aside personal funds into a private medical savings account of your own.

As you probably already know, Medicare (administered by the Social Security Administration) "kicks in" at age 65. It consists of two parts, namely A (hospital services) and B (medical services). But neither Medicare A nor B pays for everything. As a result, Medicare supplement policies may be needed. In this chapter, we want to describe these matters in an informative way, and even dangle before you the benefits of being *self-insured* in your old age. Among the benefits is a tax deduction for the medical expenses you pay for out of your own pocket.

Allowance of Deduction

The medical expense deductions that are allowable on your tax return (Schedule A, Form 1040) are prescribed by Section 213 of the Internal Revenue Code. This section is titled: *Medical, Dental, Etc., Expenses*. It consists of several subsections, the most telling of which is subsection (a): *Allowance of Deduction*. Therefore, for the purposes of this chapter, we quote this one-sentence subsection to you as follows:

> *There shall be allowed as a deduction the expenses paid during the taxable year, not compensated for by insurance or otherwise, for **medical care** of the taxpayer, his spouse, or a dependent . . . , to the extent that such expense exceed 7.5 percent of adjusted gross income.* [Emphasis added.]

These statutory words, as succinct as they are, highlight four qualifying elements for deductibility of your medical expenditures. The four qualifying elements are:

1. The expenses must be for the medical care of you, your spouse, or a dependent.
2. The expenses must be paid by you during the taxable year.
3. The paid expenses must be reduced by any insurance reimbursement you have received (or will receive).
4. The after-insurance expenses have to be further reduced by 7.5% of your AGI.

All medical expenses go on Schedule A (1040): *Itemized Deductions*. There are also six other items that go on the same schedule. Consequently, before you can get any net tax benefits for your medical expenditures, all Schedule A items together must exceed the standard deduction for your filing status.

"Medical Care" Tax Defined

Subsection 213(d) defines "medical care" as—

Amounts paid—
*(A) for the **diagnosis, cure, mitigation, treatment, or prevention** of disease, or for the purpose of **affecting any structure or function of the body**,*

(B) for transportation primarily for and essential to medical care referred to [above],

(C) for qualified long-term care services,

(D) for insurance (including amounts paid as premiums under part B of [Medicare . . . and] *supplemental insurance for the aged) covering medical care,*

(E) for lodging (not lavish or extravagant) while away from home primarily for and essential to medical care . . . provided by a physician in a licensed hospital (or in an equivalent medical care facility), and

(F) for medicine or a drug or biological which requires a prescription of a physician for its use by an individual.

There you have it. We have boiled the applicable tax law down to its essential elements. The qualifying key determining medical care is found in the empowerment words: **diagnosis, cure, mitigation, treatment, or prevention of disease, or affecting any structure or function of the body.** This pretty much includes any form of care prescribed by a reputable physician in any health specialty.

Inherently included are organ transplants, body-part replacements, tooth implants, artificial heart and breathing apparatus, licensed nursing care, wheelchairs, ambulance hire, eye glasses, hearing aids, crutches, artificial limbs, hospital beds (and accessories), electric lifts, prescription medicines and drugs, corrective devices . . . the works! Excluded are expenditures for ordinary hygiene and first aid, cosmetic surgery, family swimming pools, and vacation travel for alleged medical reasons.

No Cosmetic Surgery

To make sure that you don't get carried away with overclassifying your expenditures, other subsections of 213 impose some common sense limits. Among these are:

There shall be—
no significant element of personal pleasure, recreation, or vacation in the travel away from home . . . [and such] *amount . . . shall not exceed $50 for each night for each individual.*

By limiting medical travel to lodging only, the statutory message is that ordinary meals are not considered medical care. The exception would be special food and diet that are an inseparable part of the diagnosis, cure, etc. prescribed by a physician.

Elsewhere, subsection 213(d)(9) specifically excludes cosmetic surgery by mandating that—

(A) The term "medical care" does not include cosmetic surgery or other similar procedures, unless . . . necessary to ameliorate a deformity arising from, or directly related to, a congenital abnormality, a personal injury resulting from an accident or trauma, or disfiguring disease.

(B) The term "cosmetic surgery" means any procedure which is directed at improving the patient's appearance and does not

meaningfully promote the proper function of the body or prevent or treat illness or disease.

As an instructional summary, we depict "all of the above" in Figure 9.1. We've gone to the effort of presenting the statutory clauses because you'll find that they appear in variant words in insurance contracts, both government and private. Therefore, if what you think is a medical expense is not clearly covered by Section 213, there is no point in your spending money on it through insurance or otherwise. It is better to spend this portion of your budget on other retirement needs.

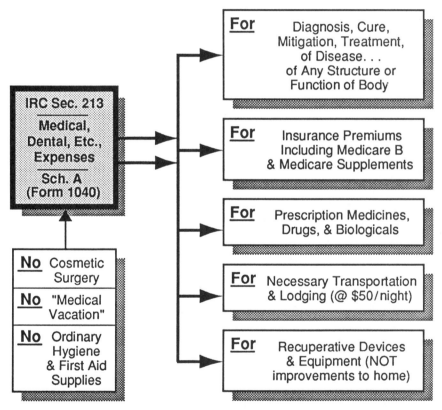

Fig. 9.1 - Expenditures for "Medical Care" as Defined by Tax Code

Subtract Insurance Reimbursements

Let's go back to subsection 213(a) for a moment. The phrase that we want to call your attention to is—

not compensated for by insurance or otherwise.

What do you suppose this phrase means?

It means several things — all implied. First of all, it means that, if you have insurance that covers a medical expense incurred, you must claim reimbursement as applicable. It makes no difference who paid for the insurance: you, your employer, the government, or some community agency. In some cases, you have to prepay the expenses before you can claim reimbursement. In other cases, you can claim the reimbursement first, then pay the unreimbursed amount later. Filing medical insurance claims can be as bad as filing tax returns. Irritations, hangups, and controversies occur. Nevertheless, you must file your claim and get a response — yea or nay — before *any* expenses are allowable.

The second meaning implied is that you must have *paid* for the medical care during the taxable year for which you are filing your return. This is not evident from the insurance phrase, but it is evident in the phrase which immediately precedes it, namely:

the expenses paid during the taxable year.

You are only allowed to deduct what you actually paid, whether before or after reimbursement.

There is still a third meaning implied in the insurance phrase. It is that, after paying for the expense (or expenses), you must *subtract* the amount of insurance reimbursement received (or credited to your account). This is where matters get a little sticky. You pay in one year, and get reimbursed the next; what happens? Or, you paid several bills to different medical providers, and made several different claims throughout the year. Some reimbursements were received in your taxable year; others were received in the subsequent year. Now what happens?

This is where the IRS gets its hook into you. Its regulation on point is **Reg. 1.213-1(g)(1):** *Reimbursement for expenses paid in prior years.* It says—

> *Where reimbursement from insurance or otherwise, for medical expenses is received in a taxable year subsequent to a year in which a deduction was claimed on account of such expenses, the reimbursement **must be included in gross income** in such subsequent year **to the extent attributable to** (and not in excess of) deductions allowed under section 213 for any prior taxable year.* [Emphasis added.]

The phrase: *not in excess of,* means the net tax benefits derived in a prior year after taking into account the 7.5% AGI threshold and your standard deduction.

The 7.5% AGI Threshold

Again, let's go back to subsection 213(a), and focus on its very last clause, to wit:

> *to the extent that such expenses exceed 7.5 percent of adjusted gross income.*

Adjusted gross income (AGI) is that amount which appears on the very last line on page 1 of your Form 1040. You are aware, of course, that this line includes the taxable amounts of your pensions, annuities, IRA distributions, **and** your social security benefits. If you have any subsequent-year reimbursement for previously paid medical expenses, your AGI includes that amount, too.

If you are a wealthy retiree (over $35,000 by IRS/SSA's means-testing standards), can't you see that your social security benefits increase your AGI? Obviously, the greater your AGI, the less medical expenses you'll be able to deduct on Schedule A. For example, if your AGI is $35,000, you stand to lose $2,625 ($35,000 x 0.075) of your after-reimbursement medical expenses. If your AGI is $50,000, you'll lose $3,750 ($50,000 x 0.075).

The Schedule A form does not let you forget about this 7.5% AGI subtraction factor. It's right there on the face of the form, as we depict in Figure 9.2. Just as we have done in Figure 9.2, the official form converts the 7.5% to its fractional equivalent: 0.075. The official form also says that, after subtracting the 7.5% AGI, if the result is zero: *Enter -0-*. If this is your result, it means that you get no medical expense deduction whatsoever. If your result is greater than zero, you still have one other obstacle: the standard deduction.

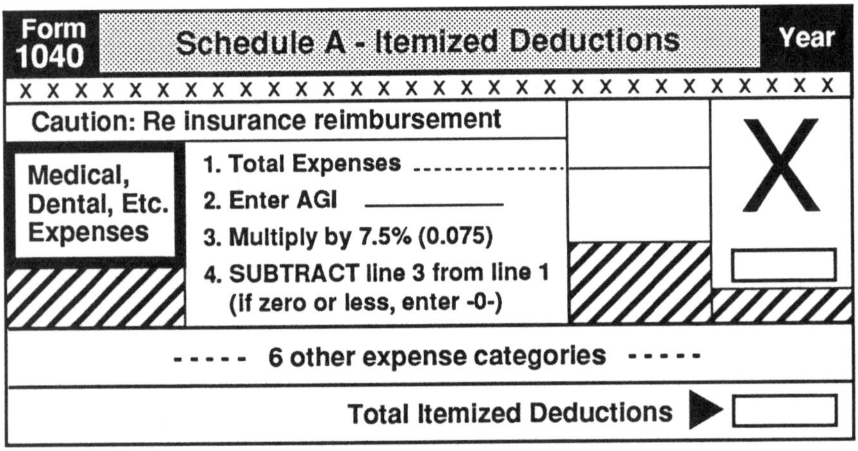

Fig. 9.2 - Where Medical Expenses Are Claimed on Your Tax Return

The Standard Deduction

After figuring your AGI, you have the choice of taking *either* (a) itemized deductions, or (b) the standard deduction. Choosing itemized deductions requires the completion of Schedule A, Form 1040. Besides medical expenses, there are six other categories of deductions (not shown in Figure 9.2) that go on Schedule A. If you have significant "adjusted" medical expenses (after insurance and after the 7.5% AGI), you have to run through your other deductions to see if your total exceeds the standard deduction. If not, there is no point in itemizing.

For taxpayers over age 65, the standard deduction runs the gamut of from about $4,000 to approximately $10,000. It depends on your filing status: single, married joint, married separate. If married, it also depends on whether one or both of you are over 65, and whether either of you is blind.

At the top of page 2 of Form 1040, filing status matters are brought to your attention. You are asked to—

Check if: ☐ *You* were 65 or older, ☐ *Blind;*
☐ *Spouse* was 65 or older, ☐ *Blind*

Add the number of boxes checked and enter the total here ▶ ☐
Go to page _____ [of instructions] *to find your standard deduction.*

For example, the standard deduction for a married couple filing jointly in 1997, both over 65 and not blind, would be approximately $8,500.

Editorial Note: The standard deduction is adjusted each year for inflation. This is why we use the qualifier "approximately."

Obviously, if your adjusted medical expenses plus your other itemized deductions on Schedule A total less than your standard deduction, you might as well forget claiming any medical expenses.

As a rough rule of thumb, unless your *after-insurance* medical expenses exceed 25% of your AGI, there is no point in claiming any medical expense deductions. Claim the standard deduction (if otherwise appropriate) and do not report as income any insurance reimbursement whatsoever. Simply divide your AGI by 4 to arrive at an amount above which your medical expenses are major. These are the expenses you want to tax deduct.

Medicare A: Tax Prepaid

Throughout your working years, you paid medicare premiums whether you wanted to or not. It was that "medicare tax" portion of those withholdings by your employer, or by yourself when self-employed. This tax was separate and distinct from your social security tax. Although both taxes were collected together by the

IRS, the SSA separated them for trust fund accounting. The social security trust fund is a separate accounting entity from the medicare trust fund.

What was probably not clear to you during your working years is what the medicare tax (insurance premiums) covered. Those premiums were to cover you for Medicare — Part A . . . only. This is the *hospital services* portion of the medicare program. It provides for partial payments for a semi-private room in a hospital, plus the general nursing, services, and supplies therewith. It includes blood transfusions, but only after you pay for the first three pints thereof.

The term "hospital services" **excludes** the cost of attending physicians, special surgery (such as organ transplants), and special medications and treatments (such as for Alzheimer's disease and cancer). These you have to pay for yourself or through other supplemental coverage.

In a nutshell, Medicare A covers the following hospital stays:

• First 60 days	All but (about) $700
• 61st through 90th day	All but (about) $175 a day
• 91st through 150th day	All but (about) $350 a day
• 151st day and thereafter	None

In addition, Medicare A covers "approved amounts" for skilled nursing care up through 20 days, and hospice care when physician-certified as being terminally ill.

For social "safety net" purposes, Medicare A is a noble and worthy program. It provides basic coverage for ordinary emergency care. It is comforting to know that you have already prepaid for this basic service, which you hope you may not need.

You are automatically eligible for Medicare A when you apply for social security benefits at age 65 and thereafter. It is effective on the first day of your birth month for the application year. Affirmation of your eligibility is signified by a Health Insurance Card issued by the SSA. The card shows your name, sex, claim number, entitlement coverage, and effective date. It is a good idea to carry this card with you at all times when away from home. No hospital can refuse admission to you if you have it.

Medicare B: You Pay

The national medicare program consists of two parts, namely: A and B. Part B (Medicare B) covers certain *medical* services whether associated with hospital stays or not. Specifically, medical services are those rendered by physicians (of all specialties), therapists, diagnosticians, nutritionists, clinical technicians, and necessary medical equipment. If "medicare approved," it also covers skilled nursing for home health care.

After the first $100 per person per year of medical services are paid by you, Medicare B *generally* pays 80% of **approved amounts**. The catch here is what constitutes a medicare approved amount. The SSA has a massive handbook of every conceivable medical service that can be rendered to humans, with assigned rates based on negotiated averages nationwide. For example, suppose after your hospital stay under Medicare A coverage, various physicians billed you for a total of $25,000. Of this amount, probably only about $16,000 would be medicare approved. It is this approved amount — not the billing amount — on which 80% would be covered by Medicare B. In other words, of the $25,000 actually billed you, Medicare B would cover $12,800 ($16,000 x 0.80). The uncovered $12,200 must be paid either by you, by other insurance, or by the acceptance of a lower fee by the billing physicians.

Unlike Medicare A, **you** have to pay the premiums for Medicare B. You paid no tax towards this coverage during your many working years. So, when you begin paying for Part B at age 65 or later, you are truly paying premiums on government administered health insurance. As health insurance premiums go, Medicare B rates are quite nominal. You pay approximately $50 per month per person.

But there's a catch. (Isn't there always?) When you apply for social security benefits at age 65 or after, you are asked if you want Part B coverage. It is not mandatory that you take it. If you do not take the B coverage, you are asked to sign a Statement that—

> I do not wish to apply for Medicare B coverage. I understand that I will be penalized with a higher premium payment if I apply for such coverage later.

The "penalty" is a lump-sum prepayment of all premiums from your post-65 age back to age 65.

Medicare B coverage is based on the concept that *all* social security beneficiaries from age 65 on are in the plan until they die. It is for this reason that the premiums are automatically withheld from each month's social security benefits. Obviously, if one declines Part B coverage until he attains age 70, 75, or later, he has not paid the same cumulative premiums that others have paid for the same coverage. He could have saved or spent the equivalent premium money elsewhere. This would give him an economic advantage over his peers. Hence, the Medicare B penalty is a form of arm-twisting to take the coverage.

Medicare Supplements: A-J

Most major nongovernmental health insurers offer "medicare approved" supplemental plans. These plans are standardized to kick in when medicare kicks out. To be eligible for any of these plans, you must be covered by Medicare A **and** by Medicare B. This is another form of arm twisting to get all seniors (65 and over) into a flexible form of universal health coverage.

There is a total of 10 different government-approved (federal and/or state) supplemental plans. They are designated consecutively from A through J. The A and B supplements dovetail directly into their Medicare A and B counterparts. These A and B supplements extend hospital stay from 150 days up to 365 days, or up to a lifetime; they extend skilled nursing from 20 days up to 100 days, or more; and they pay the 20% medical services which are medicare approved but not paid by medicare.

Supplements C through J add services which are not covered by Medicare A and B. They include preventive medical care, at-home recovery services, basic prescription drugs, extended prescription drugs, foreign travel, the first three pints of blood, surgical supplies, special equipment, and other items. The coverage in each of plans C through J differs, depending on what you perceive your major illness is likely to be.

After enrolling in Medicare A and B, you have the right to buy one or more of the A-J supplemental plans for up to six months, regardless of your health. If you forgo this right, you have to wait up to six months after enrollment in order to "phase out" any pre-existing medical conditions you may have. Once enrolled, however, your coverage cannot be canceled unless you fail to pay the premiums or are guilty of misrepresentation.

Self Insurance: Unthinkable?

If you have dealt with government agencies and insurance companies before, you know that any claim — no matter how reasonable, accurate, and straightforward it may be — is a test of your will and perseverance. Big Government and Big Corporations all behave the same. They want you to dot every "i", cross every "t", and meet every letter of the fine print in the "contract." Even then, processing a claim does not mean that it will be approved and that you will be reimbursed the proper amount. This is why a whole new cottage industry has grown up, just filling out and processing health insurance claims.

If you have the time, patience, and love the claims processing challenge, go to it.

However, there **is** another option. Should we dare mention it? It is . . . SELF INSURANCE. Is this too unthinkable?

Think about it for a moment. If you are a "wealthy retiree" — defined by the IRS/SSA as having an AGI over $35,000 — could you not pay for your own medical expenses as you incur them? Is this such a terrible thing to do on your own? The national trend is more and more towards having wealthy retirees bear their own health care freight. So, why not pay all of your medical expenses? Then you could forget about Medicare B and all Medicare Supplements A through J.

How much would it take? How much would you have to set aside into a self insurance fund of your own? Congress started thinking about this in 1996 when it enacted IRC Section 220: *Medical Savings Accounts* (MSAs).

An MSA is an IRA-like account with a self-paid insurance deductible of about $5,000 per year per family. The qualifying MSA set-aside would be approximately $3,750 per year. Together, these amounts total $8,750 per year. Let's assume that you will live to age 85. That's 20 years past the medicare starting age of 65. Thus, the amount you would need to set aside for a self-insurance pool would be

$8,750/yr x 20 yrs = $175,000

You may already have this amount or more as equity in your home. If not, you probably (in your pre-retirement planning goals) have savings and investments that would cover this amount. If not, you could probably work part-time and add to whatever set-aside pool you already have. Our point is that for some retirees who have been fortunate and prudent, self insurance is not too unthinkable

Nursing Home Care

One of the great worries of all retirees, wealthy and nonwealthy alike, is how will they pay for nursing home care when their time comes (if it comes). A nursing home is when you reach that point in life where you need help performing normal daily activities, such as eating, dressing, and going to the bathroom. Government statistics (U.S. Department of Health and Human Services) estimate that two out of every five retirees will spend time in a nursing home. Half will spend six months or less (due to death), and the other half will spend an average of two and a half years. About ten percent stay longer than five years. Seven years seems to be the very maximum. The cost of nursing home care is NOT COVERED by medicare, but can be partially covered by medicare supplements.

Nursing home care costs on average about $3,000 per month. That's $36,000 per year. Let's assume the worst case scenario of seven years in a nursing home. The cumulative amount required would be

$36,000/yr x 7 yrs = $252,000

This is not too different from our self-insurance pool above, especially when considering that the "average stay" is less than three years.

Our point is: You can have all of the medicare-type insurance policies you want, you still have to set some amount aside from which to pay certain medical expenses on your own. No insurance will cover everything. You surely know this.

Private Home Nursing

If you've never visited a nursing home to see family members and friends, you should do so now. It is a somber and depressing experience. It tears your heart out to see elderly human beings, many of whom have had successful careers, in a rapidly deteriorating physical/mental state. Most are cripple or deformed; many suffer from Alzheimer's disease, Parkinson's disease, or some form of cancer; their speech, hearing, or eyesight are gone (or nearly so); some or all of their teeth are conspicuously missing; all are on medication; and some are heavily sedated. If you've made the visit during your healthier years, you'll want no part of nursing home care in your twilight years.

A better alternative is private nursing in your own home. You have all the facilities that you are accustomed to, plus you'll do better with private attention and care. The cost will be about the same. This is because your lower home maintenance costs will be offset by higher private nursing costs. Whatever the cost, you are in your own home with surroundings that are familiar, no matter what the nature of your illness may be.

In home health care servicing, chances are your medical-type expenses would exceed 25% of your AGI. If so, claiming these expenditures as medical deductions on your tax returns makes sense. So much so that there could be some years in which your federal and state income taxes would be zero. The savings in tax could help offset various insurance premiums that you might otherwise have paid.

The hiring of private nurses and other domestic help embarks you into another tax domain. You become an **employer**. As such, you have to file a special schedule and attach it to your annual Form 1040 or 1040A. We are talking about **Schedule H** (1040): *Household Employment Taxes (For Social Security, Medicare, Withheld Income, and Federal Unemployment Taxes)*. This tax schedule is required whenever you pay **any one** household employee $1,000 or more in any given year. The schedule also requires that you make state unemployment contributions, and endure the hassle of forms and threats from state agencies. The bottom line on Schedule H is designated as: *Total Household Employment Taxes.* (This amount excludes state unemployment contribution and state withholding requirements.) You pay the Schedule H amount along with your other payments to the IRS.

Instead of Schedule H, you may prefer to employ private nurses and household workers as *independent contractors.* Talk to your own tax advisor about this matter. An experienced advisor may provide you with a simple contract form that you can use, so that the workers truly are independent. They work for others besides you. In this case, all you will need to file with the IRS is the once-a-year **Form 1099-MISC:** *Nonemployee Compensation.* It's then up to each 1099 recipient to pay his/her own social security, medicare, and income taxes.

Another way is to hire your private nurses and household workers through licensed registries or temporary-help agencies. These registries and agencies do all the employer paperwork and tax forms filings. They send you a monthly bill for all services rendered. The advantage here is that you will have replacement nurses and workers on tap at all times.

To summarize the above, we present Figure 9.3. Which of the three options you use depends, of course, on cost, the nature of your illness or disease, and whether or not you can get a close family member to manage and supervise the "hired help" for you.

Durable Power of Attorney

There is one final area of health care that we must address. We all fear the day when we may be in a coma, a state of senility, or afflicted with a terminal illness where heroic medical activity is required to keep us alive. The cost for doing this can be prohibitive; it could devastate our finances and leave our heirs destitute. To forestall this devastation of others, one can appoint a *health care agent* to make all medical decisions, even the final one . . . "pulling the plug."

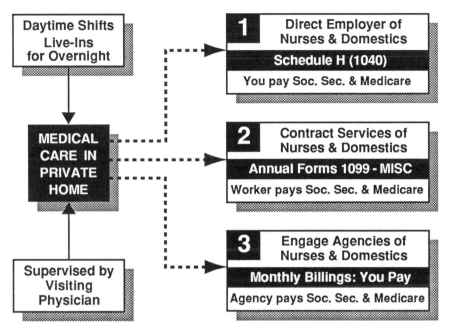

Fig. 9.3 - Hiring Options for Private Medical Care in Home

This is where a **Durable Power of Attorney for Health Care** comes in. This is a formal legal document prepared under the state law where you reside. In the document, you can express such wishes as:

☐   I do **not** want my life to be prolonged, and I do **not** want life-sustaining treatment to be provided or continued if the burdens of the treatment outweigh the expected benefits.

☐   I want my life to be prolonged and I want life-sustaining treatment to be provided **unless I am in a coma** which my doctors reasonably believe to be irreversible.

If requested, most physicians will provide you with a preapproved legal form with blank lines, checkboxes, and signature spaces. No attorney is necessary. The blank legal form has already been prepared by attorneys representing the Medical Association to which your doctor belongs.

Durable powers of attorney for health care are generally valid for seven years. This is about the maximum length of time that any human being would be in a full-care nursing facility before death. The document must be signed by the retiree creating it, and he must be capable of understanding what he is signing. He must do the signing in the presence of a notary public or in the presence of two witnesses. At least one of the two witnesses must not be related to the retiree by blood, marriage, or adoption, and must not be a beneficiary of any part of his estate.

A durable power can be revoked or renewed at any time. However, a duration clause therein reads:

> If I am unable to make health care decisions for myself when this power of attorney expires, the authority I have granted to my agent will continue until the time when I become able to make such decisions for myself.

This clause is the very reason why the term "durable" attaches to the legal title of the document.

10

ESTIMATED TAX: 1040-ES

Paying Estimated Tax Is A New Self-Assessment Process For Most Retirees. It Requires PREPAYMENTS In Four Separate Vouchers Known As "1040-ESs." Due Dates Are April 15, June 15, September 15, And January 15. On April 15 (National Tax Day), You Close Out The Preceding Calendar Year And Immediately File Voucher 1 For the Current Year. Although The IRS Provides A "1040-ES Worksheet Package," A Simpler Way Is To Use The "Safe Harbor Round Up" Rules. Voucher 4 (Due January 15) Causes Confusion And Errors With Overlapping Years. By Ignoring Voucher 4, the IRS Will Dun You A Penalty 1/2 of 1% . . . Or So.

Most persons entering retirement will face a different time frame with respect to "paying their taxes." They will be switching from withholdings of taxes to estimated taxes. The withholdings are done regularly on each pay period by one's employer. The process is as automatic as day and night. There's no thinking or scheduling on the employee's part.

When retired and receiving pension and annuity income, or IRA distributions, not all plan administrators will do withholdings. Those that do will rarely do it for different states that you may move to and retire to. Banks and brokers make no withholdings on your savings, investments, and transactions unless you specifically request in writing that they do so. The Social Security Administration ordinarily does no income tax withholdings on benefits paid to you. But this may change in the future.

Thus, there is a whole new taxpaying framework that you will have to deal with in retirement. This is the matter of estimated taxes . . . and *prepayments* thereof. The prepayments are made on entirely separate tax forms — called: *vouchers* — from those which you have been accustomed to in the past. If you've been self-employed, you will have already been exposed to the voucher forms. They are officially titled: **Form 1040-ES:** *Payment Voucher.*

Once in retirement and the 1040-ESs become your tax modus operandi, you are on your own. There is nothing automatic any more. You have to figure out your tax for the entire year **in advance,** then prepay that estimated amount in *four* vouchers throughout the year. The prepayment due dates are "odd ball"; they do not relieve you of filing your regular return after the close of the tax year. There is no doubt about it: the 1040-ESs require extra effort on your part.

Who Must File ES Forms

When the subject of estimated tax and ES forms is broached to those who are about to retire, or who have just recently retired, the reaction is universal. It goes something like this:

"Why do I have to do that? I pay any tax due when I file my return on April 15th. Why do I have to prepay the tax? The government doesn't prepay me my refunds. Besides, I can earn interest on that prepayment money. I just don't get it."

If you've heard about estimated taxes before, have you not reacted in a similar way, when first informed of your "duty" to prepay?

Therefore, it is proper to ask: Who must file Forms 1040-ES . . . and why?

The "why" is easier to answer. It is because the IRS, its instructions, the tax code, and Congress say so. Later, we'll give you the statutory and regulatory background on this.

In the meantime, the "who" part is best answered by quoting the IRS instructions for Forms 1040-ES. The key such instructions are:

*You must make estimated taxes if you expect to owe, after subtracting your withholdings and credits, at least $500 for the tax year [$1,000 commencing in 1998]. You are also required to make estimated payments if you expect your withholdings and credits to be less than **the smaller of**:*

1. 90% of the tax shown on your current year's return, or
2. 100% of the tax on your previous year's return, or
3. 110% of the tax on your previous year's return if its adjusted gross income [AGI] *is $75,000/$150,000* [depending on your filing status].

If none of your retirement income is subject to withholding, the general tripwire for ESing is $500/$1,000 or more. This amount of federal income tax corresponds to an AGI of about $10,000/$14,000 for single persons and to about $16,000/$20,000 for married persons. These ES thresholds are pretty low down on the economic scale, whether retired full time or not.

If you are working part-time for an employer, you may be able to avoid making ES prepayments. To try this, ask your employer to take out your estimated additional tax as part of his regular withholdings. You'll have to give him specifics in this regard by filing a new Form W-4: Employee's Withholding Allowance Certificate. Or, you can make the same request (on Form W-4) to your pension or annuity plan payer who does withholdings regularly.

But, there's a practical limit to asking your withholders to pay your ES taxes for you. It may be that your part-time earnings and/or your pension or annuity income are not enough to cover all of your ES tax prepayments. This is especially likely where your *nonwithholding* sources of income exceed 50% of your AGI amount. In other words, there may be no way of avoiding those ES prepayments if your AGI crosses the social security taxation thresholds presented previously in Chapter 7.

There is punitive irony in all of this. You may have to prepay estimated tax on your social security benefits long before you know how much of those benefits will be taxed.

Format & Filing Dates

You are probably itching to see what a 1040-ES payment voucher looks like. If so, we accommodate you in Figure 10.1. As tax forms go, it is a very simple format.

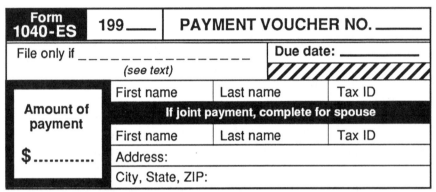

Fig. 10.1 - Prepayment Voucher Form 1040-ES (Slightly Edited)

The first impression you should get from Figure 10.1 is that big black box in the lower left portion of each 1040-ES. Think of it, if you will, as the "big black hole" of government. (Yes, we're being cynical.) Boiled down to 1040-ES essentials, all the IRS wants is money — your money. Even though your Form 1040/1040A return is not due until April 15 following the close of your tax year, the IRS wants your money ahead of time. They want it paid as your current year unfolds.

In order to give you (your "account," that is) proper credit for your prepayments, you are expected to enter your name, social security number (Tax ID), and address. If married, and filing return jointly, add your spouse's name and Tax ID, too. Joint estimated tax payments are accepted as standard procedure.

However, you may **not** file a joint 1040-ES if you are separated from your spouse under a decree of divorce or separate maintenance. Nor can you file jointly if either you or your spouse is a nonresident alien. In these separation cases, each spouse must file his/her own 1040-ES.

Also note, in Figure 10.1, the little headnote which we have indicated as: "File only if _____." The full (official) text of this headnote is:

*File only if you are making a payment of estimated tax. Return this voucher with check or money order payable to the "**Internal Revenue Service**." Please write your social security number and "199___ Form 1040-ES" on your check or money order. Please do not send cash. Enclose, but do not staple or attach, your payment with this voucher.*

In the far upper right-hand corner of Figure 10.1, a calendar year due date is indicated. We purposely left the due date blank. This is because there are **four** ES due dates each year. Because four vouchers are involved, each voucher displays a bold-printed sequence number (which we also left blank in Figure 10.1). The four voucher numbers and due dates are:

Voucher **1**	---------------	April	15, 199**Y**
Voucher **2**	---------------	June	15, 199**Y**
Voucher **3**	---------------	Sept.	15, 199**Y**
Voucher **4**	---------------	Jan.	15, 199**Z**

By all means, take care to note that Voucher **4** is due on January 15 of the year *following* the close of your taxable year. We differentiate this by showing your current tax year as 199**Y**, and the following year as 199**Z**. Voucher **4** causes a lot of recordkeeping confusion. It is NOT the first prepayment for calendar year "Z"; it is the fourth prepayment for calendar year "Y". Make sure that you understand this, and organize your prepayment records accordingly.

Confusion Over Due Dates

Of all tax matters that retirees have to contend with (except possibly IRA distributions and social security taxation thresholds), nothing is more repetitively confusing than those 1040-ES vouchers. The four different due dates screw up all natural thinking and mental-calendar processes.

In our due dates listing above, note that Voucher 1 for 199Y is due on April 15. This is the exact same date that your complete tax return for 199X is due. In other words, on April 15, you close your tax account for year "X"; and you immediately (simultaneously) start your prepayment account for year "Y". When your year "Y" final return is due on April 15, 199Z, you start Voucher 1 all over again for year "Z".

All income taxing *states* **also** require ES voucher prepayments that coincide with the IRS's due dates. (For state illustration purposes, we'll use California's Franchise Tax Board — FTB — which prescribes Forms 540.) This means, typically, that there are FOUR payment checks to be prepared on April 15 by ES taxpayers. These checks are:

Check No. 1, 199X — to IRS for Form 1040/1040A, year "X"
Check No. 2, 199Y — to IRS for Form 1040-ES(1), year "Y"
Check No. 3, 199X — to FTB for Form 540/540A, year "X"
Check No. 4, 199Y — to FTB for Form 540-ES(1), year "Y"

Nobody likes to pay taxes; most people hate it. They get emotionally distressed, particularly on April 15. So, what happens?

In the emotional stupor, check 3 is sent to the IRS (instead of to the FTB); check 2 is sent to the FTB (instead of to the IRS). Check 1 is sent in place of check 3, and check 4 is sent in place of check 2. Or, checks 1 and 2 get transposed, as do checks 3 and 4.

Any erroneous check sent to the IRS is assigned to one big collective "Unclaimed Account." It is never returned to the sender. What is returned to the sender is a statement that the form itself was received . . . but without a check. The statement also includes a demand for payment, plus (of course) penalties and interest. This is not the way honest government is supposed to work.

After the April 15 national due date, continuing with the 1040-ES vouchers (and the corresponding state ES vouchers) can be irritating. If not irritating, it is distracting. It is distracting because the subsequent due dates (June 15, September 15, January 15) are "odd ball." The timespan between April 15 and June 15 is 60 days; between June 15 and September 15 is 90 days; between September 15 and January 15 is 120 days; and between January 15 and April

15 is 90 days. How is a retiree who is approaching senility and his twilight years going to remember these days?

Even those who can remember well, will find these odd-ball dates an interference with their activity plans: travel, special projects, volunteer work, investment transactions, elective health care, and so on.

Our suggestion is to "fumble along" the best way you can. Figure out a way to make your ES voucher schedule simple. One way to do this is to file Vouchers 1 and 2 together on April 15; file Vouchers 3 and 4 together on September 15. This way, there are only two dates to remember and schedule for. One is the "national tax day" (April 15) which you can't not remember. September 15 is when Congress is in session after its summer vacation. This date also should be easy to remember.

We present in Figure 10.2 a graphic depiction of all four ES due dates, and the "overlapping" of the national due date. As indicated, try focusing your ES efforts on April 15 and September 15 only. The September date, being nine months into your current year, gives you a good handle on what your tax accountable income has been, and is likely to be for the year. Use this date to make any adjustments (increase or decrease) to your total prepayments.

Statutory Backhandedness

Strangely enough, the estimated tax requirement was never affirmatively initiated by Congress itself. It was initiated by the IRS back in 1954 by its T.D. 6119 ("T.D." is "Treasury Decision") proclamation. At that time, estimated taxing was directed primarily at self-employed individuals and nonresident aliens who were not subject to any form of withholdings. The substance of T.D. 6119 was that—

> *The payment of any installment of the estimated income tax shall be considered payment on account of the income tax for the taxable year for which the estimate is made. The aggregate amount of the payments of estimated tax should be entered upon the income tax return for such taxable year as payments to be applied against the tax shown on such return.*

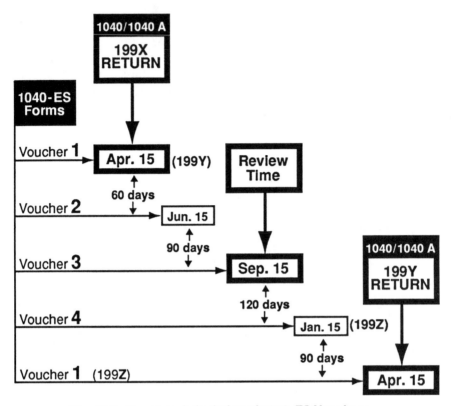

Fig. 10.2 - Due Date Scheduling of 1040-ES Vouchers

It was not until 1960 that Congress enacted IRC Section 6015: Declaration of Estimated Income Tax by Individuals. Over the years since, Congress has amended Section 6015 seven different times, finally repealing it in 1984 and replacing it with Section 6315. The latest version of Section 6315 now reads:

> *Payment of estimated income tax, or any installment thereof, shall be considered payment on account of the income taxes imposed by subtitle A* [Income Taxes] *for the taxable year.*

This one sentence is the full text of Section 6315. Do you see any imperative and mandatory wording to the effect that: "An estimated tax shall be imposed"?

Contrast the Section 6315 words with words in Section 1: Tax Imposed. Of the several subsections of Section 1, each starts off with—

*There is **hereby imposed** on the taxable income of every* [individual] . . . *a tax determined in accordance with the following table:* [Emphasis added.]

Actually, there is no direct "shall be imposed" estimated tax. Backhandedly, however, there is a "shall be added" additional tax for: ***Failure by Individual to Pay Estimated Income Tax.*** This is the title of Section 6654 which was added to the tax code in 1986. Its subsection (a): Addition to the Tax, reads—

*In the case of any underpayment of estimated tax by an individual, there **shall be added** to the tax under* [subtitle A] . . . *for the taxable year an amount determined by applying—*

(1) the underpayment rate established under section 6621,
(2) the amount of the underpayment,
(3) for the period of the underpayment. [Emphasis added.]

Thus, even though there is no mandatory law imposing an estimated tax, there is a penalty mandate (addition to tax) for underpaying the estimated tax. Since the IRS is a penalty-hungry bureaucracy, there is no escape option other than trying to do the best you can to estimate your prepayments conscientiously.

A Simple Estimating Way

The IRS has available a 1040-ES Worksheet Package for first-time filers of estimated tax. The package is a 6-page set of instructions, separated into 12 parts, followed by a 17-line worksheet, topped off with the threat of penalty if you don't make your prepayments timely and in sufficient amounts.

Rather than using the 17-line worksheet and becoming upset with the penalty threat, there **is** a simpler way. The key is to discipline yourself to **two dates:** April 15 and September 15.

On or before April 15, you must complete and file your regular tax return (Form 1040/1040A) for 199X. Schedule yourself to do this at least 10 days before the deadline. This gives you ample time to get your ES vouchers ready. For the "first cut" at your estimated tax for 199Y, use the 199X amount. Then apply a "gut factor adjustment" (GFA). Adjust your 199X tax amount up or down in proportion to any increase or decrease in income that you expect for 199Y. If in doubt, use the same tax amount as for 199X. Then round up to the next higher amount evenly divisible by 4. For example, suppose your tax for 199X was $12,690. Round this up to $12,800. When divided by 4, each of your payment vouchers comes out to $3,200. Always make your voucher payments in even dollar amounts. There is less chance that the IRS will screw things up for you.

If, as a result of selling your home, taking a lump-sum pension or annuity settlement, or divesting a large block of your investments, there will be a balloon increase in your income stream. In this case, multiply your 199X tax by 110%, then round up and divide by 4 as above.

If, as a result of retiring or other significant decreases in income, multiply your 199X tax by 90%. Then round *down* and divide by 4 as above.

File Vouchers 1, 2, and 3 with your GFA-1 adjustment regularly and on time. Voucher 3 is due on September 15, 199Y. By this time, you should have a good handle on what your tax accountable income has been or is likely to be, for the year. Now, you make a GFA-2 adjustment. But, this time, make it *down* (if applicable): **not** up. Do this for Voucher 4 only. If your income stream for the year appears as though it will be 25% (or so) *less* than that which you anticipated on April 15, disregard Voucher 4 altogether. Don't send it in. There is nothing the IRS can do to you.

Once you get the knack of our simplified procedure, it will work like a charm, year after year. Why are we so sure? Because we are using the safe-harbor rules for avoiding the underpayment penalty.

There are three safe-harbor rules that you should memorize . . . and apply. They are:

☐ 90% rule: 90% of the tax on your current year's return

☐ 100% rule: 100% of your prior year's tax
☐ 110% rule: 110% of prior year's tax when significant increases in current year's income

We depict the application of these rules in Figure 10.3. They apply only for your ES prepayment vouchers when filed on time. They are designed to avoid the irritation and nuisance of underpayment penalties.

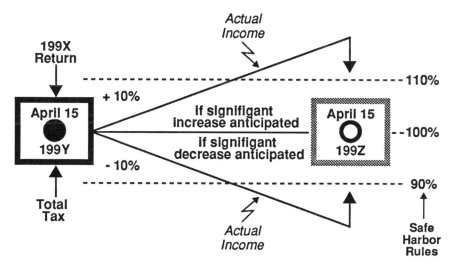

Fig. 10.3 - Simple, Safe Way of Estimating Tax for ES Vouchers

Penalty Is Foregone Interest

There is a special reason why the IRS wants your ES voucher money long before April 15. It turns the money over to the U.S. Treasury Department which either spends it or invests it to earn interest. Either way, it deprives you of earning interest on it. Technically, your tax for 199Y is not officially due until April 15, 199Z. Yet, you have to pay a penalty for each ES voucher that is late or underpaid.

In reality, the ES underpayment penalty is not all that severe. It is the mildest form of all penalties that the IRS loves to impose. Structurally, it is the equivalent of foregone interest that the U.S.

Treasury doesn't earn on your ES money. It is a *fractional year* type of interest that applies to each ES voucher separately. The base interest rate is that which the IRS applies to all late tax payments per annum. Typically, these annual rates vary from 6% to 10% (depending on inflation).

Let us illustrate the general magnitude of the foregone interest penalty. To show this, let's take a "worst case" scenario. You decide NOT to make any ES prepayments, preferring instead to pay all of your tax for the closed year on April 15. Assume that the applicable IRS interest rate is 8% (0.08). What is the maximum penalty that can be imposed for each voucher due date? (Note: The letters TTD used below stand for "Total Tax Due" on April 15).

Answer:

Voucher 1 — 100% x 0.08 x 1/4 TTD = 0.020 TTD
Voucher 2 — 85% x 0.08 x 1/4 TTD = 0.017 TTD
Voucher 3 — 60% x 0.08 x 1/4 TTD = 0.012 TTD
Voucher 4 — 25% x 0.08 x 1/4 TTD = <u>0.005 TTD</u>
Total for the year = 0.054 TTD

In other words, if you paid absolutely no ES tax for the year, and paid it all on April 15, your foregone interest penalty would be slightly over 5%. Of course, if your TTD is $10,000 or more, 5% of that amount is $500 or more that you would be throwing away. Our recommendation is: Pay at least three vouchers, then stop.

If you did not pay Voucher 4 at all, what would be your foregone interest penalty? Answer: about 1/2 of 1% of your TTD (assuming all conditions above).

We are trying to convey to you an important psychological and character-building message. Do not let the IRS psyche you out and force you into overpaying your tax with its threats of ES penalties. Pay Vouchers 1, 2, and 3 on time, and skip the fourth one. If there is any penalty — and there may *not* be — let the IRS bill you for the 1/2 of 1% Voucher 4 interest. Chances are, the "penalty" would not run more than $10, $20, or so . . . hardly worth fretting over. If enough retired taxpayers disregarded Voucher 4, it would be a great character-building movement against the IRS bureaucracy.

Self-Crediting Your Return

Aside from being a little mischievous about it, there is a practical reason for our urging you not to pay Voucher 4. Ordinarily, this voucher is due and payable on January 15, 199Z. The payment, however, is credited to your 199Y year: not 199Z. This one voucher alone is where all the ES prepayment credit screw-ups occur. It's a mental mixup thing — not senility — caused by two overlapping years. It happens to everybody, young and old alike . . . *including* the IRS.

Our solution is: Ignore Voucher 4 altogether. If this troubles you, pay Voucher 4 in the same calendar year that you pay Vouchers 1, 2, and 3. At least your records will be in calendar year order when you go to prepare your final return for the ES prepaid year.

Form 1040 / Form 1040 A		Page 2

Tax Computation, Credits, & Other Taxes

(A) **Total Tax** ▶ [   ]

PAYMENTS	● Withholdings .... _____ ● ES payments .... _____ ● Other payments ..... _____

(B) **Total Payments** ▶ [   ]

If. . . **(B) > (A)** **Overpayment** **(A) > (B)** **Underpayment**	● Overpayment [ ] Towards next ES. . . [ ] Refund ⟶ [ ] **AMOUNT DUE** ● Underpayment [ ] ES tax penalty. . . [ ]

> means "greater than"	**Signature Block**

Fig. 10.4 - The ES Payments Credit Portion of Form 1040 / 1040A

Whether you file Form 1040 or Form 1040A, on page 2 thereof, slightly more than midway down, there is a line entry which reads—

This is your total tax. ▶ _____

To help orient you as to where we are, we present Figure 10.4. It is edited and abbreviated, but it shows you the key lines that we want to discuss from here on.

Below the "total tax" line (in Figure 10.4), there are various credit lines, such as withholdings, ES prepayments, and other credits and payments. With regard to your ES payments, there is a separate line of its own which reads—

199Y estimated tax payments and amount applied from 199X return _____

Then, after subtracting this and other payments and credits from your total tax, you arrive at either an overpayment amount **or** an amount due. Your official forms show this with bold-printed lines

If you have overpaid your tax, you are given the opportunity to apply all or part of it to your 199Z tax. Or, you can take all or part of your overpayment as a refund. If the overpayment is $500 or more, apply it towards your 199Z estimated tax and make up any difference on Voucher 1. If it is less than $500, claim it as a refund and pay Voucher 1 as if there were no overpayment. Overpayment amounts less than $500 tend to get lost in the "computer clutter" of the IRS's paperwork processing.

11

NONRESIDENT STATE RETURNS

You May Desire To Move To A Retirement State Different From Your Working State. When Such Move Happens, And Income-Producing Property Is Left Behind (Whether Real, Tangible, Or Business) You Are Faced With Filing A NONRESIDENT (Or PART-YEAR RESIDENT) State Tax Return. If You Have Property In Several States, You Face Multiple Nonresident Returns. If You Retire To A Taxing State, You Also Face "Double Taxation" Concerns. Limited Relief Through Tax Credits May Apply. If You Retire To A Nontaxing State (There Are 9), You Are NOT Relieved Of Paying Tax To Your Nonresident States. Only Selling Or Exchanging Properties Provides Relief.

Potentially, one of the most irksome retirement matters that you may have to address has to do with nonresident state returns. A "nonresident state" is one in which you are not living, but in which you own income-producing *property*. Most often, such property is real estate. It could be residential rentals, commercial buildings, farmland, natural resources, recreational land, or other realty. It also could be tangible property such as vehicles, machinery, equipment, merchandise (inventory), or leasehold improvements used in a trade or business. Whether real or tangible, if it produces income, and the state in which it is located imposes an income tax, you will have to file a *Nonresident Return* for that state.

Many persons with modest and above-modest means tend to move from state to state within the U.S., interspersed with temporary residencies overseas. This "moving around" is particularly true in the early years of retirement. The motivation is to settle in at one location central for maintaining contacts with family, friends, investments, and travel interests. The objective also is to find a place with comfortable weather, reasonable housing, low crime, and convenient medical facilities. In one's occupationally active and career-building years, these objectives were less important than they are now.

Unless one has had outstate property interests while occupationally active instate, the concept of filing nonresident state returns is new to most retirees. Residency principles and nonresident taxation theory introduce a whole area of decision making which we've not previously discussed. We want to point out some of these matters to you and give examples of how you could be affected.

State Residency Principles

There is no universal law which spells out exactly what constitutes residency in a particular state of the U.S. Each state promulgates its own residency requirements for enjoying the benefits and suffering the burdens within its boundaries. By far, most residency requirements focus on conditions for asserting income taxation authority over individuals and entities. Generally, these conditions relate to time and intent. Since California is the most populated state in the nation (nearly 32,000,000 inhabitants), its residency laws serve as useful guidelines for experiences you may have missed during your peak money-making years.

California law defines the term "resident" to include:

1. *Every individual who is in the state for **other than a** temporary or transitory purpose.*

2. *Every individual who is domiciled in the state but who is outside the state for a temporary or transitory purpose.*

3. *All individuals who are not "residents," as thus defined, are "nonresidents."*

The terms "residency" and "domicile" are not the same. A domicile is an individual's permanent home. It is the place to which, whenever absent, he intends to return. One may be domiciled outside California, and still, by remaining in the state for other than temporary or transitory purposes, be considered a California resident. Conversely, California domiciliaries may not be considered California residents if they remain outside the state for purposes that are not temporary or transitory.

Hence, the key for establishing residency or nonresidency is what constitutes "temporary or transitory." There are no hard and fast rules. When taxation powers are at issue, the theory is advanced that—

*the state with which a person has the **closest connection** during the taxable year is the state of his residence.*

The term "closest connection" relates to time in state, and the presence of active sources of income.

Generally speaking, if you have a permanent home outside of California and you visit the state for less than six months, and while so visiting derive no income, you are regarded as being instate for temporary or transitory purposes. But, if you visit and stay *more than nine months*, you are **presumed** to be a California resident. Once so presumed, you are subject to California income taxes on your sources of income . . . **worldwide!**

Residency laws, community property laws, and state income tax laws are very important when deciding where to live in retirement. Said laws also are important for determining what forms of income property to keep, if the property is located outstate from one's domicile. We present several examples below to illustrate the kinds of questions that can arise.

Spouses in Different States

Once the retirement process is underway, it is not uncommon for each spouse to want to live in a different state from that of the other. Such desire has nothing to do with marital disharmony. It could be that each wants to be nearest his or her early roots. Or, it could be that each wants to be nearer different children and grandchildren. It could be that their recreational activities are diametrically opposed: he likes fishing; she likes symphony. Or it could be that one wants to stay put, while the other wants to explore new ventures and income opportunities. Whatever the reason, there is agreement that the two spouses will travel back and forth frequently to visit with each other. Even so, some situations regarding residency preference can lead to an impasse.

Take the case of a working couple who reached their retirement years at about the same time. They had a permanent home in California. The husband's brother lived in North Carolina where both brothers inherited several hundred acres of land in a developing community. The husband decided to move to North Carolina, buy a home there, and "supervise" the subdivision, development, and sale of his co-owned land. The wife wanted to stay in California where her mother and daughter lived.

At this point, the retiree couple had two homes: one in California and one in North Carolina. Both California and North Carolina are income-taxing states. Each state deemed the couple to be residents of its state. When it comes to income-tax time for filing in April, which of the two state returns do they file?

Answer: They file resident returns for both states!

Whether they file married separately or married jointly, they pay essentially the same tax to both states.

California says that because the couple are California residents, they pay tax on income generated in North Carolina. In turn, North Carolina says that because the couple are also residents of North Carolina, they pay tax on income generated in California. Isn't this "double taxation," you ask?

Yes, it is. And there's no relief. One's state of residence governs his taxation liability. Ordinarily, a residence state will grant a limited credit for taxes paid on the same income to another state. This "other state" credit applies, however, **only if** the other state is a nonresident state. In the situation above, neither California nor North Carolina is a nonresident state. The consequence: a double taxation impasse.

After the first double-tax filing year, the impasse was resolved. The couple gave up their California residence by "selling" (and partially gifting) their home there to their daughter. North Carolina became their sole residence state. Still, they retained visitation rights with their daughter in California. Taxwise, North Carolina was the logical residence choice. There was long-term retirement income from subdividing and selling off residential and commercial building lots. Why would anyone pay tax to California for land sold in North Carolina?

Part-Year Residency

The above real-life example points up another retirement decision matter. State residency is not established or disestablished automatically. Nor is it an exact beginning-of-year or end-of-year matter. It is a part-year phenomenon. Even one day in a given taxable year constitutes part-year residency.

The year in which you change residency from one state to another is your "transition year." This means that you can be a part-year resident in State A (your departing state), and also a part-year resident in State B (your arriving state). But you have to signify which part is which, to each state separately. How do you do this?

Answer: By filing a part-year resident return with State A and — separately — filing a part-year resident return with State B.

All income-taxing states have two versions of their annual tax returns. There is a full-year residency version and a part-year residency version. Needless to say, the part-year version is the more complicated one. It is so because you have to allocate your *federal* sources of income worldwide into its instate and outstate components. What is instate for State A is outstate for State B, and vice versa. The general scheme is as we depict in Figure 11.1.

All taxing states these days, whether for a full-year or part-year resident, start their forms by referencing your federal AGI (Adjusted Gross Income). You itemize every source of your federal income, then establish which portion was instate and which portion was outstate. It is not a matter of the number of days instate or outstate; it is the number of actual dollars generated in each state separately. For example, you could have been in State A for 15 days, yet could have sold a piece of property there which netted you $50,000. That would be State A income: no proration to State B.

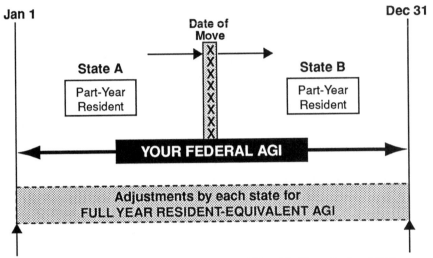

Fig. 11.1 - Instate/Outstate Allocation of Taxable Year Federal AGI

Each state has its own instructions on what to include and what not to include as a part-year resident. Often, the instructions are ambiguous.

For part-year residency, the intermediate computational goal is to establish your residence *ratio* for that year. That is, your

$$\text{Residence Ratio} \; = \; \frac{\text{Part-Year AGI}}{\text{Full-Year AGI}}$$

The "full-year AGI" is that state's equivalent of your federal AGI, as though you'd been instate for the full year.

Most states require that your residence ratio be computed to four decimal places: _._ _ _ _. An example would be 0.3456. Although generally less than 1.000, your residence ratio could actually be greater than 1 (e.g. 1.0125).

Each state's part-year return directs that you first enter that state's tax as though you were a full-year resident. After doing this, you apply your residence ratio to arrive at the part-year tax. For example, assume that the full-year resident tax is $1,686. Using the 0.3456 ratio above, your part-year tax would be—

$1,686 x 0.3456 = $583

As you'll see later, the same AGI ratio approach is used for computing your nonresident tax, should you retain income property in the state from which you have departed.

When Leaving a State

Once they have decided to pull up stakes, many retirees overlook — sometimes intentionally — the departing state tax requirements. If you've been a resident of a taxing state for 20 years, say, and you depart without filing a part-year return, what do you suppose will happen?

For the first year or two after your departure, probably nothing will happen. This gives you a false sense of security. By the third year or fourth year, you'll be contacted by the income taxing agency of your former residence state. You'll be declared a delinquent taxpayer for Year X . . . for Year Y . . . and probably also Year Z. For each of these years, you'll be assessed a full-year's resident tax, based on your federal AGI for each of your absent years. It will be the maximum tax possible, plus penalties and interest (of course). If you departed from California, we guarantee that this **will** happen to you. California is an aggressive taxing state.

In 1995, a divorced retiree quitclaimed his California home to his ex-wife, and moved to Texas (a nontaxing state). In Texas, he sold $83,638 worth of hi-tech stock for which he net gained only $138. He dutifully reported this on his federal return and totally ignored California. About 18 months later, he was sent a *Notice of Proposed Assessment* by the FILING ENFORCEMENT Division of the Franchise Tax Board, Sacramento, CA. The billing read:

Tax liability	*$ 7,900*
Penalty for late filing	*1,975*
Penalty for failure to file upon demand	*1,975*
Interest (to date hereof)	*765*
Filing enforcement fee	*75*
Total Tax, Penalties, Interest, and Fee	*$12,690*

The notice went on to say—

We sent you a notice previously that we have no record of a 1995 California personal income tax return being filed. You are required to do one of the following within 30 days:

- *File a 1995 California return, or*
- *If you have already filed, send us a copy, or*
- *Provide proof that you are not required to file.*

Otherwise, this assessment becomes final, due, and payable 60 days from the date hereof.

Subsequently, the delinquent retiree filed his 1995 part-year California return in 1997, showing a total tax due of $160. His penalties and interest came to $100. This version is a long way from the arrogant state demand for $12,690. California, it turned out, treated the $83,638 gross stock sales as 100% ordinary income.

The moral here is obvious. When you leave a taxing state to take up residence elsewhere, file on time a part-year resident return. File even if you were only in that state for one day of the taxable year. File even if you owe only one dollar. Otherwise, how do you inform the taxing state that you are no longer subject to its jurisdiction?

Residency Questions

All taxing states (there are 41) have a residency questionnaire form. The questionnaire is not on the full-year resident return; it is on the part-year/nonresident return only. This means that you have to know about (and specifically request) the part-year residency form on your own. It is not automatically sent out every time you change address, or move out of or into a different state. State revenue agencies simply don't track you on their own. They track you through the IRS.

Thanks to the *Electronic Information Superhighway*, all but two states of the 50 (Nevada and Texas) have entered into "agreements of cooperation" with the IRS. The purpose of these agreements is to exchange information on the identity and income of persons who have failed to file **either** federal or state tax returns. Whichever taxing agency (federal or state) gets the information first, electronically transfers it to the other agency. This was all sanctioned by Congress in 1976 when it added Section 6103(d) to the Internal Revenue Code: *Disclosure of Return Information to State Tax Officials.*

Our point is that, just because you are retiring, you are not exonerated from your tax filing chores. You must procure and answer each state's residency questionnaire form with care. The residency questions are directed at one of three situations, namely:

- Part-year residency, departing
- Part-year residency, entering
- Nonresident for full year

If married, the residency questions must be answered separately for each spouse.

Using California as an example, the type of residency information sought is abbreviated in Figure 11.2. Note that the questions are in two parts: *during* current year and *before* current year. The "before" current year information is to enable the state to go through your tax filings — and nonfilings — of the past, to dun you for any delinquent taxes. This is a subtle warning to get all of your tax returns in order, before departing a resident state.

Ordinarily, a state taxing agency has four years to dun you for any erroneous or incomplete filings you may have made. But if you do not file when required to, there is no time limit to hounding you. Consequently, we cannot overstress the importance of timely filing a "departing resident" state return. **Do so** . . . whether you owe any tax or not. Make it clear that you've left the state.

Incidentally, most states' departing resident returns are identified as *Nonresident or Part-Year Resident* returns. Our suggestion is that you memorize this nomenclature. Since you do not file the return until after the close of the calendar year in your new resident state, it is easy to forget the special form required. The key identifying word is **Nonresident**. This is the case even though you initially may be using the form for part-year purposes.

RESIDENCY INFORMATION QUESTIONNAIRE		Year	
Name(s) as shown on return		Your SSN	
		Spouse SSN	
		Yourself	Spouse
DURING Current Year			
1	Became resident of California on... (enter date of move & prior state of residence)		
2	Became nonresident of California on... (enter date of move & new state of residence)		
3	Was nonresident of California for entire year (enter state or country of residence)		
4	Number of days in California (for **ANY** purpose)		
5	Owned home or property in California (enter "yes" or "no")		
BEFORE Current Year			
6	Was California resident for the period... (enter dates)		
7	Entered California on... (enter date)		
8	Left California on... (enter date)		

Fig. 11.2 - California Questionnaire for Residency and Taxation

When You Become "Nonresident"

Once you are out of a prior residency state for a full year or more, you are a *nonresident* thereof. If you have no property (realty or business) or tangible income sources left in the departing state, you have no further tax obligations to that state. However, if you left any real or tangible property, and it generates any income, either annually or at time of its sale, you have a nonresident return to file with that state. That is, provided that the state you left is a taxing state. There are 41 income taxing states in the U.S. Each has its own return forms and checkbox questions for residency, part-year residency, and nonresidency.

At this point, recall in Figure 11.2 Question 5. It more generally reads—

Did you own a home or property in _____ (state) _____ ?
Enter "Yes" or No".

The term "property" includes any form of real or tangible property that is capable of earning income throughout the year, or capital gain/loss at time of its disposition. The term does **not** include pensions and annuities, IRA accounts, bank accounts, investment accounts, and the like. These are "intangible assets" which attach to the residence of the owner: not to the physical location of their custodian.

The most common situation when retirees move out of state is that they tend to retain their home there for a few more years or so. They do this because they are not sure that they will stay out of state. After a year or two, or three, they may want to come back. Or, they have adult children or elderly parents who need a place to live. Or, sometimes they may rent the vacant home to close friends for a nominal fee, for "housesitting" and defraying maintenance costs, utilities, and mortgage payments. In these situations, it is not until the home is sold that it becomes a tax reportable event.

All real estate sales in the U.S. are broker reported to the IRS on **Form 1099-S**: *Proceeds From Real Estate Transactions*. The gross proceeds only are reported: not the net gain or loss. Form 1099-S shows the date of closing, *your* name and address — and Tax ID — wherever you may be living at the time.

There is an obvious purpose to Form 1099-S. It is to impose on you the duty to report the transaction on a nonresident return, to the state where the property was physically located. If you do not do so in a timely manner (by April 15 of the year following the date of closing), the nonresident state will delinquent tax you on the full gross proceeds . . . plus penalties and interest.

If, for example, your home sold for $500,000 and you failed to report the sale on that state's nonresident return form, you're in for a horrible surprise. You would likely be assessed anywhere from $65,000 to $80,000 in nonresident state tax. The assessment would stand, even if your actual gain were only $10,000 or you suffered a loss.

How does a nonresident state collect its assessment when you are out of state?

Four ways, actually. One, through its cooperative agreements, it takes — or tries to take — your federal and resident state income tax refunds. Two, it engages a private collection agency in your resident state to come after you. And, three, it attempts to record a tax lien on your property, if any, in your resident state. When it comes to the recording of tax liens on instate property by an outstate authority, not all states cooperate with each other wholeheartedly. And, finally, if all else fails, when you die, the nonresident state makes a probate claim against your gross estate. This action deprives your heirs of some — maybe all — of their after-probate inheritance.

Nonresident Taxation Principles

Nonresident taxation is serious business. It is far more so these days, because of Internet communications and exchange agreements between the IRS and state taxing agencies. To a reasonable person, taxing the income from physical assets located within a nonresident state seems plausible enough. What is not so reasonable is how nonresident taxation works. It is not just identifying one's nonresident income and paying the nonresident tax on that amount alone. It is more complicated than this. In effect, you pay proportionately on your resident state income as well as on your nonresident income. Let us explain.

First off, nonresident taxation starts with your federal AGI. No matter what state you reside in (whether taxing or nontaxing) you have to file a federal return. To the federal AGI, **two** adjustments are made. We call these adjustments Class I and Class II. Class I adjustments are for differences between federal and state law, as though you were a full year resident of the nonresident state. Class II adjustments are those which specifically identify the Class I items as being nonresident income.

Class I adjustments are made because not all federal sources of income are identically taxable by the states. For example, social security benefits are federally taxed but not by most states. Interest income from U.S. Treasury Obligations, while taxable by the IRS are not taxable by states. State tax refunds are IRS taxed, but not by the refunding state. And so on. The federal-state differences are usually well known to residents, but less well known to nonresidents. The Class I adjusted gross income is the equivalent of decreeing that a nonresident is a resident for tax purposes. This is your first indication that ordinary logic breaks down.

Class II adjustments are those which separate your nonresident income from your resident-equivalent income. In most cases (with good records) expressly identifying your nonresident income is not too difficult. There can be some uncertainties with dividends and capital gains. After all proper adjustments have been made to your resident-equivalent income, you arrive at your nonresident income.

All nonresident state returns have their own version of an "Adjustment Schedule." We generalize such a form for you in Figure 11.3. The idea is to show the sequential adjustments across columns A, B, C, D, and E from federal sources of income to nonresident state sources of income. Note the two "Totals" blocks: resident-equivalent income and nonresident income. These two totals are used to establish your *nonresident income ratio*. We show the ratio in the lower portion of Figure 11.3.

How the Ratio Works

Let us illustrate how the nonresident income ratio works. We'll use simple numbers: $10,650 for your nonresident AGI (Column E in Figure 11.3) and $45,000 for your resident-equivalent AGI (Column C in Figure 11.3). With these amounts, your nonresident ratio becomes

$$\frac{10,650}{45,000} = 0.2366$$

The nonresidence rules require that you apply this ratio to the amount of tax on the resident-equivalent income of $45,000. Let's assume that the nonresident state is California; that you are a single person retiree; and that the taxable year was 1996. If the $45,000 were your California *taxable* income (instead of your California AGI), the state tax would be $2,608. Multiplying this amount by 0.2366, your nonresident tax becomes

$$2.608 \times 0.2366 = \$617$$

Income Item	Federal Gross	Class I Adjustments	Resident Equivalent Income	Class II Adjustments	Nonresident Income
	A	B	C	D	E
1 Interest					
2 Dividends					
3 Cap. gains					
4 Business					
5 Rents					
6 Pensions					
7 IRAs					
8 Soc. Sec.					
X Other					
Totals ▶					

Representative Adjustment Schedule for Nonresident Returns

$$\text{Nonresident Ratio} = \frac{\text{Col. E}}{\text{Col. C}} = \frac{\text{Nonresident Income}}{\text{Resident-Equivalent Income}}$$

Fig. 11.3 - Nonresident Source Income Derived From Federal Gross Income

Common sense would suggest that you pay nonresident tax only on your nonresident income of $10,650. If this were indeed the case, your tax would be $165. Thus, the nonresident state (California in our example) gains another $452 (617-165) in tax revenue. In effect, California is biting into your non-California income . . . and loving it.

Suppose you retired to a nontaxing state. (There are nine such states: Alaska, Florida, Nevada, New Hampshire, South Dakota, Tennessee, Texas, Washington, and Wyoming.) Would California or some other nonresident state still get $452 out of your resident state income?

Yes, it would! No matter how close you fine tune your nonresident state return, you'll always pay a higher tax through the "ratio process" than a straight tax on the same nonresident income.

In other words, even if you paid no resident state income tax, the nonresident state where you held property would still get a big percentage bite out of your resident state income.

Other State Tax Credit

It is not uncommon, especially in your early years of retirement, to have nonresident sources of income in one, two, or three states. The most likely is where you were formerly a resident in the now nonresident state, and you retained property there. A second likelihood, with more time on your hands, is that you invested in a partnership, S corporation, co-venture, or other business entity operating in a nonresident state. A third likelihood, which happens quite often, is that you inherited property (say a farm, timberland, or oil and gas leases) from your parents or other relatives who lived in a nonresident state. As a result, the situation could well be as we depict in Figure 11.4.

If you retire in a taxing state as your state of residency, the Figure 11.4 situation would cause multiple double-tax headaches for you. Most resident taxing states allow a *limited credit* for the taxes paid to another state on the double taxed income. It is the **resident** state that allows this credit: not the nonresident state. This is because resident states, by precedent and law, assert jurisdiction over all of your income worldwide. Nonresident states assert jurisdiction only over your property owned and services performed within their state borders.

How is the credit for income taxes paid to a nonresident state claimed?

Each resident state has its own claim forms. The identifying term most frequently used is: ***Other State Tax Credit***. You are first required to identify all double taxed sources of income. Then you are instructed to compute a tentative credit with two alternative formulas. The formulas are—

$$(1) = \frac{\text{Double taxed income by resident state}}{\text{Resident state adjusted gross income}} \times \text{resident state tax}$$

$$(2) = \frac{\text{Double taxed income by nonresident state}}{\text{Nonresident state adjusted gross income}} \times \text{nonresident state tax}$$

The allowable credit is the *lesser of* the two computed amounts.

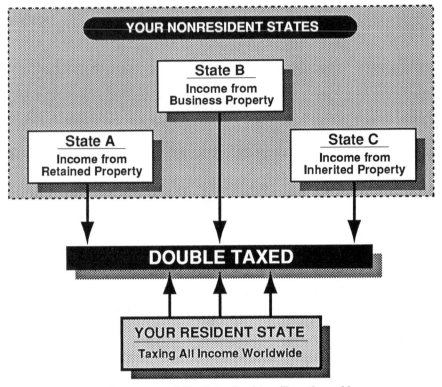

Fig. 11.4 - Prospects of Multiple Double - Taxation of Income

The formulas are set up by the resident state to take advantage of the tax rate differentials between the states, and differences in state laws for adjusting the federal AGI to its state equivalent. In other words, if you reside in a high taxing state, your credit will be limited to that of the lower taxing state. If you reside in a low taxing state, you'll not get full credit for the tax paid to the high taxing state.

After a few years in retirement and filing nonresident returns, you may reach a point where you decide to clear out all nonresident sources of income. You may also decide to retire in one of the nine states (identified on page 11-14) which do not tax individual incomes.

12

YOUR FULFILLMENT YEARS

> After The Transitional Decisions Come A Series Of Minor Decisions For Enhancing Retirement Fulfillment. This Is That Special Period Known As THE GIFT OF TIME In Your Life. Use It To Clear Out Household Items, Update "Cost Basis" In Investments, Sell Portfolio Clutter, Reduce Realty Holdings, And Sanitize Your Financial Estate Via The RULE OF THREE. In the Process, Routinize Tax Filings, Minimize Trusts (And Contacts With Attorneys), And Build A Cash Hoard To Make Life Simple And Free. Spend Your Time AND Money On a Worthwhile Cause, Project, Or Niche As Your Memorial To Others.

Our overall premise is that retirement itself is a transitional phase. It is a time for major decisions to be made when changing from one lifestyle to another. After working 30, 40, or 50 years in an active occupational career, one cannot make all retirement decisions overnight. They must be made thoughtfully and deliberately because . . . there's no turning back.

To go through the transition into retirement right takes from three to five years. This is what the previous chapters have been all about. But after about five years, a new realization takes hold. There is a need to simplify life in anticipation of the "last transition" that you'll face. This is when you enter those twilight years when you are less and less able to make decisions on your own. In the ensuing time interval, there is a golden opportunity to be yourself

. . . and enjoy yourself. Not in a carefree travel and play style, but with meaning and purpose to life. These are your fulfillment years.

The transition years from working to retirement are comprised of multiple rather major decisions; the fulfillment years are comprised of multiple rather minor decisions. These are mundane matters such as clearing out your junk , consolidating your bank and investment accounts under the "Rule of Three," having cash on hand to give to family and charities, and having a consuming passion for some activity requiring your time, talent, and brain.

Clear Out Household Junk

One person's junk is another person's treasure. If this sounds out of place for a tax book, think again. Any pin money you earn selling the stuff is not taxable; any gifts to charity you make are tax deductible. Now is your chance to make a "win, win."

Over your 30 to 50 years of adult working and living, you have collected a lot of "things." They take up space in your household and their use value is pretty much gone. We are talking about those hand tools, power tools, garden equipment, golf clubs, ski equipment, recreational vehicles, gun collections, hunting trophies, sewing and art supplies, costume jewelry, souvenirs, odd works of art, computers and software, old shoes, used clothing, fur coats, worn rugs, beat up furniture, outmoded kitchen appliances, old china and silverware, and other trinkets and gadgets that you move around from place to place wondering what to do with them. Your fulfillment years are the time to get rid of these items. So, go to it.

How do you get rid of your household clutter collections? There are at least six good ways, namely:

Way 1   — Arrange for a "garage sale"; advertise locally; and have your children (or neighbors' children) help with the sales.

Way 2   — Contact your local "flea market"; contract with a regular vendor there; transport your "merchandise" to him on consignment; give him a commission on what he sells.

Way 3 — Contact an auction house in your area; have them pick up and inventory your items and include them in an areawide "estate sale"; the auction house will take its commission and send you a check.

Way 4 — Donate the items to a charity of your choice; get an itemized receipt for the items you have delivered or they have picked up; immediately annotate each item with its flea market value.

Way 5 — Contact one or more museums in your general area; inform them of items which have historic, artistic, cultural, or heritage value; request a written receipt with their appraisal values thereon.

Way 6 — Call a haul-away service; pay them to load and haul your unsaleable and nondonative items to the nearest community garbage dump.

In the case of Ways 1, 2, and 3, you are getting money from the sales; any tax consequences here? Absolutely none. Pocket the money or bank it. It is *not* tax accountable. It is not personal service income; you didn't make any profit either. All items that were sold were for less than what you paid for them. There is no sales tax for you to collect. Your selling effort was incidental and not part of an ongoing regular business of yours.

In the case of Ways 4 and 5, if any single item was worth $250 or more, you must get a separate receipt and appraisal estimate from the donee. A receipt is needed for each such item. If, collectively, the items donated exceeded $500 in value, you must prepare Form 8283: *Noncash Charitable Contributions*, Section A. If any single item was worth more than $5,000 (such as an antique car, vintage piano, computerized pipe organ, parcel of land), you must get a professional appraiser to sign Section B, Part III: *Certification of Appraiser*. After this documentation, you claim the valued items as "Gifts to Charity" on Schedule A of your Form 1040. There's an entry line about midway down which says: *If over $500, you MUST attach Form 8283*.

Update Basis in Investments

In your pre-retirement days, you probably attended a number of free seminars on investments in stocks, bonds, mutual funds, limited partnerships, and exotic derivatives thereof. The general thesis in those seminars was to diversify your portfolio with the objective of "making up" for lost investment time in the past. The motivating idea was to enhance your discretionary retirement funds beyond that which you would get from employer plans, social security, and the equity in your home. This was a constructive objective which we fully support.

That was then. You are in retirement now — in your fulfillment years. In your eagerness to make up for financial lost time, you have probably overdiversified and lost track of your cost basis in the investments which you acquired. It is time now to resurrect and reconstruct your *basis* in each of your investment assets. The term "basis," as you know (or should know) is the cumulative amount of capital that you have invested in each asset from date of acquisition to present date. An "asset" is one or more shares (or one or more units) representing your ownership interest in an item or entity whose market value changes over time. In other words, you need to establish your "cost basis" in each separate asset that you have acquired, but haven't yet sold.

In order to establish your cost basis, you must first determine the purchase price of all the shares (or units) that you own in a particular stock, mutual fund, limited partnership, etc. Over the years, you may have purchased shares at different prices and in different amounts. In addition, you may have reinvested your dividends, capital gains, and other distributions. These reinvestments should be included in your cost basis calculations. Otherwise, you risk paying taxes twice: once when you report the distributions on **Schedule B** (1040) and again when you report the sale on **Schedule D** (1040). To establish your cost basis correctly, you'll need all of those transactional statements from your broker, and all of those Forms 1099-DIV (Dividends and Distributions) that he is required to send you at the end of each year.

Once you have all of your records collected for each separate investment, organize them chronologically (earliest date first, latest date last). Then determine your cost basis by using one of the following methods, namely:

1. The Average Cost, Single Category method
   — this allows you to average the cost of all shares in a specified issue (ABC, JKL, or XYZ) regardless of the length of time you held them.

2. The Average Cost, Double Category method
   — this allows you to designate a particular issue of shares, separate them into those which you held one year or less (short term) and those which you held more than one year (long term), and cost average them within each of the two categories: short and long.

3. The "Specific Identification" method
   — this allows you to choose which shares are sold, as long as you identify them specifically (in writing) before you sell them.

4. Request Cumulative Cost from broker
   — require broker to include all "automatic reinvestments" of dividends, capital gains, and other distributions.

It is better to do all your record gathering and sorting, and cost basis updating when you are not under any pressure to sell. Selling under pressure always increases the risk of errors in judgment and errors in computations. Furthermore, in your fulfillment years, you should know your cost basis "up to the minute" to help you decide whether you are making money or losing money when you do sell.

Sell All Portfolio Clutter

By having updated cost basis data at your fingertips, you are in position to classify each of your portfolio ("paper type") investments by their performance. That is, classify your investments as (a) good (meaning high yield), (b) so-so (meaning low yield), (c) not-so (meaning neutral yield), and (d) bad (meaning negative yield). Here, the term "yield" means total return (increase in share/unit value *plus* all distributions over your entire holding period) divided by the number of years held. This gives you an average annual yield for each investment. We define a good investment as one whose yield is 8% per year or more throughout your period of holding. All else —the so-so, not-so, and bad — is pure clutter. You don't need this.

Portfolio clutter not only clutters up your recordkeeping tasks, it clutters up your mind (by always hoping your investments will do better), and it clutters up the monetary value of your estate.

Clutter investments have a habit of creeping into your portfolio during your occupationally active years. You hesitate to sell them, thinking they'll do better if you hold them longer. Maybe they will; maybe they won't. But, in your fulfillment years, we're not sure that you have enough time left to find out. Your goal at this stage is to simplify your financial affairs and reduce the distractions in your life. Towards this end, our suggestion is to sell your portfolio clutter. Yes, *sell it all* — the so-so, not-so, and bad. Keep only your good investments: those yielding 8% or more each year.

Don't listen to your investment broker, financial counselor, or family member unless he/she, too, is in his/her fulfillment years. Young (or younger) advisors have a different perspective from yours at this stage. So, don't even think about clutter selling as an investment choice. Think of it as freeing your mind — and your money — for enhancing your enjoyment of life.

By selling all of your investment clutter, there will be tax accounting for each and every item sold. However, the tax consequences will not be severe. Your biggest concern will be the detail required when reporting each item on **Schedule D** (Form 1040): *Capital Gains and Losses.* If you followed our cost basis urging above, filling out Schedule D should be — perhaps not quite — a "piece of cake."

As an aid in completing Schedule D, be sure to have at hand your copy of **Form 1099-B**: *Proceeds from Broker Transactions* on each clutter item sold. By reporting this exact amount in the "sales price" column on Schedule D, you should be spared any computer-matching hounding by the IRS. Your objective is to free up any tax headaches . . . once and for all. There is more to retirement life than trying to make an extra thousand dollars or two by holding on to clutter investments which have demonstrated less than superb performance. For a general summary of our clutter sale urgings, we present Figure 12.1. Note that the key element in the clean-up process is being able to make up your mind.

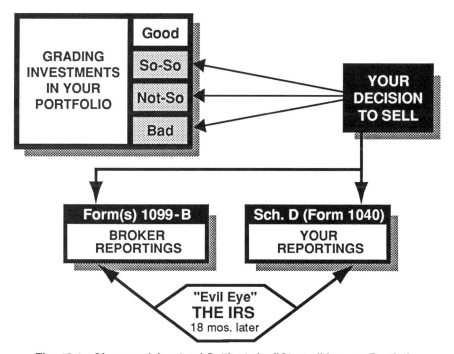

Fig. 12.1 - Characterizing (and Selling) the "Clutter" in your Portfolio

Reduce Realty Holdings

Investment greed and emotion often lead people to do unwise things, or refrain from doing wise things. This is particularly true with real estate holdings for income or investment.

There is something ancestral and emotional about owning real estate. It "gets in one's blood." A piece of land — no matter how small or large — reaches down to the earth's core. As such, it will be there forever and, therefore, can be passed down from generation to generation. But in the present environment of more government, more regulation, and more taxes, real estate — other than one's personal residence — can be more of a burden than emotional value in one's fulfillment years.

Unsold (or undisposed) real estate at time of death is the cause of much valuation controversy with the IRS. If left to its own, the IRS will always attach to each piece of real estate a value that is much higher than its true market value. This is because the federal death tax rate *starts* at 37% (for estates over $600,000) and extends up to 55% (for estates over $3,000,000). Consequently, leaving real estate, other than your personal residence, in your estate when entering your twilight years, can impose a very heavy burden upon your heirs.

If you are of a bent that has real estate in your blood, we urge that you review your holdings now. By "holdings," we mean such property as raw land, vacation land, farm land, timber land, residential rentals, nonresidential rentals, commercial buildings, boating docks, etc. Get informal appraisals or estimates, reconstruct any tax benefits (such as depreciation) you have taken, and decide on a program of reducing your holdings *before* the onset of your twilight years. The program should include some sales (cash or installment) and some gifts (noncharitable and charitable).

Excluding your residence, when you sell income-producing or business-type realty, you file **Form 4797**: *Sales of Business Property*. This form affords you what we call: *The Section 1231 Advantage*. This section of the tax code enables you to use capital-gain treatment if there is a net gain, or ordinary-loss treatment if there is a net loss. Capital-gain treatment is more tax beneficial than ordinary-gain treatment; ordinary-loss treatment is more beneficial than capital-loss treatment. Ask your own tax advisor about this.

If you gift real property to your children or others than your spouse, you must get the property professionally appraised. Then prepare a gift deed and have it officially recorded in public records. After this, file **Form 709**: *U.S. Gift Tax Return*. Unless the property value is over $600,000 (for 1997), there is no immediate gift tax. However, the amount of gift (less a $10,000 annual exclusion per donee) *will reduce* your normal death tax exclusion.

If you gift any of your realty to charity, you need to file **Form 8283**: *Noncash Charitable Contributions* and complete Section B

— Appraisal Summary, in its entirety. This requires the following subpart completions:

Part I   — Information on Donated Property
Part II   — Taxpayer (Donor) Statement
Part III   — Certification of Appraiser
Part IV   — Donee Acknowledgment

Attach this form to your regular tax return and claim the allowable amount as a deduction on Schedule A (Form 1040).

The Sanity "Rule of Three"

Our general assumption is that one does not reach his true fulfillment in retirement until age 70 and beyond. In your own case, you may back this down a few years, say from 65 on. In any event, our premise is that you want to make your tax and financial life as simple for yourself as possible. This is where our "Rule of Three" comes in. This rule is a philosophical guide for a safe, sane, and sound retirement lifestyle. If you haven't made your hoped-for millions by now, chances are you may not from now on.

The "Rule of Three" says, in effect, that you should have no more than **three active** financial accounts at any one time. This does not mean that you should not change your account custodians, when conditions warrant. It simply says that you should limit them to three . . . at any one time. Why three? Because the human mind thinks more clearly and decisively when choosing among only three options. If there are more than three accounts, say 5, 10, 15, or more, confusion and indecision set in. Either mistakes are made or no action is taken. If the idea of three-only accounts sounds naive or oversimplified, you can always have one, two, or three subaccounts associated with each of your three primary accounts.

The three types of primary accounts that we recommend are:

No. 1. Checking account — with direct deposit sweep-ins, and electronic transfer privileges.

No. 2. Savings account — with passbook, ATM, and credit card withdrawal privileges.

No. 3. Investment account — with automatic sweep-ins and money market check-writing privileges.

Our depiction of the separate functional roles of each of these accounts is presented in Figure 12.2. You could manage thousands, hundreds of thousands, and millions of dollars with just three types of accounts as depicted.

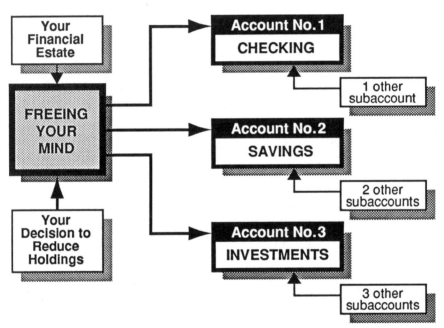

Fig. 12.2 - The "Rule of Three" for Simplifying Your Financial Life

Account No. 1 is a no-interest-bearing, checkwriting-only bank account with a federally insured banking institution of your choice. This is your sole depository account for *all* monetary funds (except investment yields) that you may receive. This funnels all noninvestment income into one place where you can, after the fact, identify its source origin (for tax purposes) more readily. Choose a banking institution that is easy to deal with, and which provides for returning all cancelled checks without request on your part.

Account No. 2 is an interest-bearing savings account for ease of consuming part of your nest egg in readily available cash form. This means having convenient physical access for passbook, ATM, and credit card withdrawals. It is the ease and security of cash withdrawals that you want for those situations where you do not want to write a check on Account No. 1. All money in this account is designated as "spendable."

Account No. 3 (investment) is where your big money is. The key to success in this realm is having a money market subaccount anchor with checkwriting privileges. You want telephone and/or electronic access to this checkwriting subaccount for switching to and from other investment accounts. Pick *one* brokerage firm or mutual fund company that offers you a good selection among investment goals. Stick with this one firm, or change to another, but do all of your active investing under one management umbrella. Whenever you want to replenish Accounts No. 1 or No. 2, do so from this account.

Routinize Tax Filings

If you have followed some of our suggestions above and in earlier chapters, you should be at a point where your tax return filings become rather routine. You've gotten any disputive matters out of the way. Hopefully, too, you have liquidated the major portion of your estate, and you are not engaging in new business ventures. You have adapted to a routine of estimated tax prepayments, and have simplified your financial accounts and investments along the lines depicted in Figure 12.2.

What is left for you now is to develop (if you haven't already done so) the necessary skills and recordkeeping procedures for preparing your own tax returns. If you have had professional preparers do your returns in the past, we think it is important that you start doing your own tax returns now. Doing so will keep you mentally alert and attuned to the tax and fiscal shenanigans of government. Who knows, someday taxpayers will gain direct referendive rights on tax and fiscal policies of government through their annual tax returns. We believe that some form of direct referendive power by taxpayers is ultimately coming. It is that "fourth power" which is yet to be recognized in the political arena. As a tax active retiree, you'll be on the forefront of a much-needed structural change in government. You should want to participate directly in this excitement.

Once you have developed the knack for doing your own tax returns without professional assistance, it is timely to consider who among family is to be your "tax assistant." You should consider such a person whether you do your returns manually or by computer. Preferably, such a person should be a generation below you who has exhibited good financial judgment, and who has demonstrated an interest in tax preparation matters. Having a designated tax assistant within your family is a prudent preparatory step for those times when you are away on travel, experiencing arthritic discomfort, or when those first signs of senility set in. Your adult children, nephews, and nieces are among your first choices. You want to have someone you can trust and who knows where your records are in time of emergency or other need.

Minimize Trusts & Attorneys

One of the most oversold facets of retirement life has to do with trusts and the various arrangements therewith. A "trust" — no matter what magic-sounding name is assigned to it — is a *legal entity* other than yourself. It is an entity into which you transfer (or may transfer) all or portions of your property (cash or noncash) to be managed and accounted for by a person or entity called "trustee." Oh, yes, you can be your own trustee . . . while alive. And this is where all of the confusion arises.

A fulfillment-years retiree who is his own trustee of his own trust has difficulty — extreme difficulty in most cases — distinguishing between the management function of his trust entity (which legally owns the property) and the management functions of his personal ownership of the same property. The confusion reaches a crescendo when tax time comes. The custodian of each item of income-producing property (savings accounts, portfolio investments, real estate) has to prepare IRS Forms 1099:

Information Returns. Does the custodian use the trust name and trust Tax ID, or does he use your name and ID? (Answer: It depends on whether you have a revocable or irrevocable trust.) No matter how you instruct the custodian on these matters, there will be computer screwups. There always are. Then the IRS will hound you with its computer matching (**CP-2000**) program. Before long, you have a tray of snakes on your table.

Trusts are oversold by attorneys, financial counselors, insurance agents, and accountants. They pitch trusts as though they are the magic key to heaven. THEY ARE NOT! Trusts **are** tax accountable entities. They save you no more taxes than you as an individual can save. In some circumstances, they *may* avoid probate (the legal passing of title to property), but probate can be avoided by other means (joint tenancy, for example).

Trusts have to be legal entities in the state where the trustor (transferor of the property) and his property reside. This requires an attorney to prepare, an attorney to interpret, an attorney to defend, and an attorney on tap when disputes between the trustee and beneficiaries arise. Attorneys — and the legal profession at large — are not known for clarity of thought, promptness of action, and modesty in fees. We urge, therefore, that you minimize contact with attorneys in your fulfillment years. Generally, they are problem creators: not problem solvers.

Where do *we* stand on trusts?

First, don't even think about trusts unless your gross estate exceeds $1,000,000 (1 million). This is your "start thinking" level — but only if your spouse is physically incapable or mentally senile, or your children and grandchildren are spendthrifts. Your "serious level" begins when your gross estate exceeds $3,000,000 (3 million). Trusts make sense from here on up because of "wolves in the woodwork," and the prudence of distributing your property to multiple beneficiaries over multiple years.

If the concept of having a trust fascinates you, contact a reputable trust preparer in your area. Tell him (or her) that you are not interested in the sales pitch. You want to know the nitty-gritty and nuts and bolts of how trusts work, and how a trust can be beneficial in *your* specific case. Tell the trust preparer that you are interested in engaging an *independent trustee* (who is not an attorney), and that you want to know what the real world will be when you are no longer around.

Prepare for Own Demise

Your fulfillment years are also the time to semi-finalize the preparations for your own demise. Your preparatory effort need not be overly detailed: just contingency-type planning. After all, our Creator has not made his final call, nor has he given any indication when he will do so. Yet, it does not hurt — in fact, it is prudent — to lay out semifinally some of your plans.

In this category of contingency planning, we suggest that there are at least six "must do" items to be agendized. These are:

    Must Do #1 — Update Last Will and Testament
    Must Do #2 — Consider Durable Power of Attorney
    Must Do #3 — Organize all tax records
    Must Do #4 — Organize all financial records
    Must Do #5 — Locate all legal documents
    Must Do #6 — Make handwritten instructions to Executor

Central to preparing for what you don't like to think about is updating your Last Will and Testament (M.D. #1). Chances are, you already have a Will, or have its intent buried in some exotic-sounding trust. If so, locate it, read it, and update it. A Will should be a separate document of its own. Do not integrate it into a trust, insurance policy, or an annuity contract. It expresses your own personal intent regarding your property, your executor, and your heirs. It is a once-only document; it has no ongoing features once your property has been distributed (including transfers into trust).

We have already discussed a Durable Power of Attorney (M.D. #2) — as "pull-the-plug" protection — back in the latter part of Chapter 9. This is a prudent contingency item where you anticipate the possibility of prolonged illness and pain.

Gathering and organizing your tax and financial records (M.D. #3 and #4), and designating a specific location in your household for them, makes good sense. Once the records are organized and updated, you'll be inclined to use them more frequently yourself.

You'll also be proud to instruct your tax assistant and executor in how well you keep them, and where they are located in case of need.

Legal documents (M.D. #5): These are your birth certificate, marriage certificate, military discharge, divorce decree, retirement letters, social security "award," life insurance policy, title deed to home, title deed to other real property, motor vehicle registration, and any pending legal matters such as lawsuits, judgments, bankruptcies, etc. Usually, these documents are in scattered locations around your household, hidden in folders, boxes, and memorabilia. You need to gather them, sort them, and put them in one place where your spouse, adult children, and designated executor have convenient access to them.

Making *handwritten* instructions to your executor (M.D. #6) takes no more than two or three pages at most. These instructions are personal things that you don't want in your Will, or in your tax, financial, and legal records. They constitute reflections on your past and preferences on how your personal belongings, artifacts, papers, and memorabilia are to be distributed . . . or destroyed. These should be in your own handwriting (for credibility reasons) rather than being typewritten or computer printed.

For orientation purposes on the role of these preparatory tasks, we present Figure 12.3. We want to emphasize that the tasks portrayed should be done by you. Don't be misled into thinking that, if you set up a trust and designate a trustee (other than yourself), said tasks will all be done by someone else. This perception is a myth.

Build a Cash Hoard

As you set about contemplating what you really want to do in your fulfillment years, there is one special task that you should promptly commence and always continue. Build up a cash hoard. Provided that you have a safe place or two for keeping it, nothing is more satisfying than having cash money — green paper — to do with as you wish.

Every so often, draw out money in the form of actual cash from your various Figure 12.2 accounts. Get it in convenient denominations and build up towards a comfortably accessible

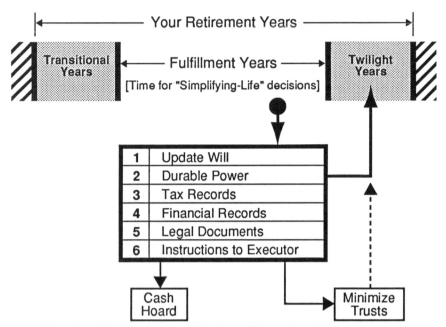

Fig. 12.3 - The Basics (and Timing) of Preparing for Own Demise

amount. For self-accounting and self-control purposes, build a cash repository up to, but no more than, about $10,000. The actual amount you build will depend on your overall financial status. As you spend down below this amount, replenish it.

Why do we pick $10,000 as the top working goal?

Answer: Because this is a suspicion level above which you are *presumed* to be engaged in some illegal activity. Once so presumed, your cash hoard can be seized by law enforcement officers and used for their own purposes. A lot of injustice has been committed by government agents just on implied suspicions regarding cash holdings. In the situation that we have presented, PLEASE DO NOT WORRY. As you withdraw the money from your various Figure 12.2 accounts, keep every single one of your withdrawal confirmations. Keep them in a separate *cash evidence* file. With this kind of evidence of where the cash came from, you have a valid counterclaim against an overzealous/overintrusive agent for his/her allegation of your being engaged in illegal activities.

What do you do with all that cash money?

Answer: You spend it! What you don't spend, you give away. Here's your chance to get a big chuckle out of life. What you spend or give away, the IRS will not get, no attorney will get, and no unworthy heir will get. This now becomes your moment of true freedom in life. You deserve it; you earned it.

Spend the money on yourself, your spouse, your children, your grandchildren, your close family members, your dear friends, and on a few of those homeless and unemployed souls who are really having a tough time making ends meet. By doing so, you are not a philanthropist; you are a pragmatist. You want to "see" where your money goes. You can't "see" where it goes in the black hole of the U.S. Treasury or into the pockets of prestigious charitable organizations which pay high administrative salaries.

And there's real glory to this spending and giving away of cash. **You don't have to keep a record of it!** Since you are not claiming any of these expenditures on your tax returns, no records are necessary. Ideally, after fulfilling your own needs and those of your spouse, wouldn't it be wonderful to be able to spend or give away every last penny up to the day of one's death? Talk about simplifying your estate, avoiding taxes, avoiding probate, avoiding attorneys — this is it! But it is also a fantasy. You should have something more constructive to do.

Pursue a Consuming Project

Surely, during your working years, there was some project or niche activity that kept flashing through your mind that you wanted to do . . . but could not find the time. It's that dream to do something constructive with your latent talents and interests. What kept you from doing so was that you had to earn a living, feed your family, and participate in an ongoing career. The dream was something that you had to put off until later. The "later" is now. Now is the time to pursue that special niche of activity that you've been thinking about all during your past years.

Maybe you like to paint; maybe you like to collect historical objects; maybe you are a railroad buff; maybe you like to make models of ships, planes, old cars; maybe you like sewing and serging (decorative overlock sewing); maybe you like genealogy;

maybe you like making tassels; maybe you like photography or interior design; maybe you like to write children's books; maybe you like to help others in times of disaster; maybe there's some endangered wildlife species you want to save; maybe you'd like to be a docent in an art, historical, archaeological, or other type museum; maybe you'd like to be a mentor to younger persons in your prior trade, business, or profession. There are a lot of "maybes" you'd like to do in life before the final curtain falls.

Whatever you've had an inkling to do over the years past, but couldn't, pursue it now with a passion. Recall and develop your latent talents, skills, and interests, and put them to use. Think of the effort, if you will, as your chance to help better mankind. You don't have to worry about earning a living anymore. Your desires for great wealth and material possessions probably have been tempered by your experiences in reality. You are free now to apply your energy and thought into helping others . . . in some way.

Other than your surviving spouse and disabled/handicapped children, if any, you have no obligation whatsoever to leave your money to anyone. Sure, you need enough to see your life through to the end. Beyond this, it is not heresy to spend and consume your money on a cause, project, or niche in which you firmly believe.

As one geriatric philosopher has said: "The GIFT OF TIME is now yours." Use it. Use *both* your time and money to engage in a worthwhile endeavor that can become your memorial to others. This is what your fulfillment years in retirement are all about.

ABOUT

THE AUTHOR

Holmes F. Crouch

Born on a small farm in southern Maryland, Holmes was graduated from the U.S. Coast Guard Academy with a Bachelor's Degree in Marine Engineering. While serving on active duty, he wrote many technical articles on maritime matters. After attaining the rank of Lieutenant Commander, he resigned to pursue a career as a nuclear engineer.

Continuing his education, he earned a Master's Degree in Nuclear Engineering from the University of California. He also authored two books on nuclear propulsion. As a result of the tax write-offs associated with writing these books, the IRS audited his returns. The IRS's handling of the audit procedure so annoyed Holmes that he undertook to become as knowledgeable as possible regarding tax procedures. He became a licensed private Tax Practitioner by passing an examination administered by the IRS. Having attained this credential, he started his own tax preparation and counseling business in 1972.

In the early years of his tax practice, he was a regular talk-show guest on San Francisco's KGO Radio responding to hundreds of phone-in tax questions from listeners. He was a much sought-after guest speaker at many business seminars and taxpayer meetings. He also provided counseling on special tax problems, such as divorce matters, property exchanges, timber harvesting, mining ventures, animal breeding, independent contractors, selling businesses, and offices-at-home. Over the past 25 years, he has prepared nearly 10,000 tax returns for individuals, estates, trusts, and small businesses (in partnership and corporate form).

During the tax season of January through April, he prepares returns in a unique manner. During a single meeting, he completes the return . . . *on the spot!* The client leaves with his return signed, sealed, and in a stamped envelope. His unique approach to preparing returns and his personal interest in his clients' tax affairs have honed his professional proficiency. His expertise extends through itemized deductions, computer-matching of income sources, capital gains and losses, business expenses and cost of goods, residential rental expenses, limited and general partnership activities, closely-held corporations, to family farms and ranches.

He remembers spending 12 straight hours completing a doctor's complex return. The next year, the doctor, having moved away, utilized a large accounting firm to prepare his return. Their accountant was so impressed by the manner in which the prior return was prepared that he recommended the doctor travel the 500 miles each year to have Holmes continue doing it.

He recalls preparing a return for an unemployed welder, for which he charged no fee. Two years later the welder came back and had his return prepared. He paid the regular fee . . . and then added a $300 tip.

During the off season, he represents clients at IRS audits and appeals. In one case a shoe salesman's audit was scheduled to last three hours. However, after examining Holmes' documentation it was concluded in 15 minutes with "no change" to his return. In another instance he went to an audit of a custom jeweler that the IRS dragged out for more than six hours. But, supported by Holmes' documentation, the client's return was accepted by the IRS with "no change."

Then there was the audit of a language translator that lasted two full days. The auditor scrutinized more than $1.25 million in gross receipts, all direct costs, and operating expenses. Even though all expensed items were documented and verified, the auditor decided that more than $23,000 of expenses ought to be listed as capital items for depreciation instead. If this had been enforced it would have resulted in a significant additional amount of tax. Holmes strongly disagreed and after many hours explanation got the amount reduced by more than 60% on behalf of his client.

He has dealt extensively with gift, death and trust tax returns. These preparations have involved him in the tax aspects of wills, estate planning, trustee duties, probate, marital and charitable bequests, gift and death exemptions, and property titling.

Although not an attorney, he prepares Petitions to the U.S. Tax Court for clients. He details the IRS errors and taxpayer facts by citing pertinent sections of tax law and regulations. In a recent case involving an attorney's ex-spouse, the IRS asserted a tax deficiency of $155,000. On behalf of his client, he petitioned the Tax Court and within six months the IRS conceded the case.

Over the years, Holmes has observed that the IRS is not the industrious, impartial, and competent federal agency that its official public imaging would have us believe.

He found that, at times, under the slightest pretext, the IRS has interpreted against a taxpayer in order to assess maximum penalties, and may even delay pending matters so as to increase interest due on additional taxes. He has confronted the IRS in his own behalf on five separate occasions, going before the U.S. Claims Court, U.S. District Court, and U.S. Tax Court. These were court actions that tested specific sections of the Internal Revenue Code which he found ambiguous, inequitable, and abusively interpreted by the IRS.

Disturbed by the conduct of the IRS and by the general lack of tax knowledge by most individuals, he began an innovative series of taxpayer-oriented Federal tax guides. To fulfill this need, he undertook the writing of a series of guidebooks that provide in-depth knowledge on one tax subject at a time. He focuses on subjects that plague taxpayers all throughout the year. Hence, his formulation of the "Allyear" Tax Guide series.

The author is indebted to his wife, Irma Jean, and daughter, Barbara MacRae, for the word processing and computer graphics that turn his experiences into the reality of these publications. Holmes welcomes comments, questions, and suggestions from his readers. He can be contacted in California at (408) 867-2628, or by writing to the publisher's address.

ALLYEAR Tax Guides
by Holmes F. Crouch

Series 100 - INDIVIDUALS AND FAMILIES

BEING SELF-EMPLOYED .... T/G 101
DEDUCTING JOB EXPENSES .... T/G 102
RESOLVING DIVORCE ISSUES .... T/G 104
CITIZENS WORKING ABROAD .... T/G 105

Series 200 - INVESTORS AND BUSINESSES

INVESTOR GAINS & LOSSES .... T/G 201
HOBBY BUSINESS VENTURES .... T/G 202
STARTING YOUR BUSINESS .... T/G 203
MAKING PARTNERSHIPS WORK .... T/G 204

Series 300 - RETIREES AND ESTATES

DECISIONS WHEN RETIRING .... T/G 301
WRITING YOUR WILL .... T/G 302
SIMPLIFYING YOUR ESTATE .... T/G 303
YOUR EXECUTOR DUTIES .... T/G 304
YOUR TRUSTEE DUTIES .... T/G 305

Series 400 - OWNERS AND SELLERS

RENTAL REAL ESTATE .... T/G 401
OWNING NATURAL RESOURCES .... T/G 402
SELLING YOUR HOME .... T/G 404
SELLING YOUR BUSINESS .... T/G 405

Series 500 - AUDITS AND APPEALS

KEEPING GOOD RECORDS .... T/G 501
WINNING YOUR AUDIT .... T/G 502
DISAGREEING WITH THE IRS .... T/G 503
GOING INTO TAX COURT .... T/G 505

All of the above available at bookstores, libraries, and on the internet

For a free 8-page catalog,
or information about the above titles, contact:

ALLYEAR Tax Guides
20484 Glen Brae Drive, Saratoga, CA 95070

Phone: (408) 867-2628   Fax: (408) 867-6466